In
memory
on
Lawrence & Sylvia Chait,
art lovers

30

30 GIRLS ON THE BRIDGE 1901

Edvard Munch

by FREDERICK B. DEKNATEL

Harvard University

with an introduction by JOHAN H. LANGAARD

Municipal Collections of Oslo

MUSEUM OF MODERN ART NEW YORK in collaboration with the Institute of Contemporary Art Boston

3781234?

Published April 1950 by Chanticleer Press, Inc.,
41 East 50th St., New York 22

The first edition of 15,000 copies was printed by
Clarke and Sherwell Limited, Northampton, England.
Design and production by Adprint Limited, London.

Contents

Acknowledgments

The undertaking which has resulted in the first major publication on Edvard Munch in the English language, and the first definitive exhibition of his paintings and prints in the United States, has been a work of devotion for scholars and statesmen on both sides of the Atlantic. Those of us most intimately concerned with the project have been overwhelmed by the many acts of friendship, courtesy and generosity which have marked its development over several years.

Principally, the action of the City of Oslo in sending so many important works abroad, to remain for an extended period, and that of the Norwegian Government, in lending a series of masterpieces from the National Gallery and appropriating public funds to defray a large share of the expense entailed in the exhibition's preparation, are recorded with a sense of high privilege and gratitude. That Munch stands today as a symbol of the growing friendship and understanding of the Norwegian and American peoples is further underscored by the altruism of the Norwegian lenders of his works and the staunch support of many friends of Norway in the United States.

We are particularly indebted to Mr. Erling Christophersen, Mr. Hans Olav, Press Secretary of the Norwegian Foreign Office, Mr. Ted Olson and Mr. Rolf Stranger for their sympathetic and expeditious handling of all official matters; Dr. Sigurd Willoch, Professor Haakon Shetelig and Mr. Lithgow Osborne for enlightened counsel and aid; and Mr. George Unger Vetlesen and the Norwegian-American Line, through whose good offices the exhibition has been brought across the Atlantic.

Research and publication have been supported largely through the very generous grants made by the Fogg Museum Fellowship for Modern Art, the Milton Fund of Harvard University and the American-Scandinavian Foundation.

For assistance in preparing the text the author's thanks are due to the librarians of the Fogg Museum, Harvard University, the National Museum, Stockholm, and the University Library, Oslo, and to Anne Bellmann, Virginia H. Deknatel, Sigrid Kjellberg, Wilhelm R. W. Koehler, Sven Liljeblad, Meyer Schapiro and Frederick S. Wight.

Frederick B. Deknatel
Johan H. Langaard
James S. Plaut
EXECUTIVE COMMITTEE

Honorary Committee

Hon. Charles Ulrick Bay	*American Ambassador to Norway*
Erling Christophersen, Esq.	*Cultural Attaché, Norwegian Embassy, Washington*
Hon. Nils Handal	*Mayor of Bergen*
Hon. Halvard M. Lange	*Norwegian Minister of Foreign Affairs*
Hon. Lars Moen	*Norwegian Minister of Church and Education*
H. E. Wilhelm Morgenstierne	*Norwegian Ambassador to the United States*
Ted Olson, Esq.	*Public Affairs Officer, American Embassy, Oslo*
Hon. Lithgow Osborne	*President, American-Scandinavian Foundation*
Professor Haakon Shetelig	*University of Bergen*
Hon. H. E. Stokke	*Mayor of Oslo*
Hon. Rolf Stranger	*Chairman of the Board, Municipal Collections of Oslo*
George Unger Vetlesen, Esq.	*New York*
Dr. Sigurd Willoch	*Director, National Gallery, Oslo*

Lenders to the Exhibition

The Municipal Collections	*Oslo*
The National Gallery	*Oslo*
The Gallery of Painting	*Bergen*
Rasmus Meyer Collection	*Bergen*
Museum of Modern Art	*New York*
Jörgen Cappelen, Esq.	*Oslo*
Thorvald Johnsen, Esq.	*Oslo*
Ragnar Moltzau, Esq.	*Oslo*
Miss Inger Munch	*Oslo*
Christian Mustad, Esq.	*Oslo*
I. B. Stang, Esq.	*Oslo*
A. M. Vik, Esq.	*Oslo*

Introduction

JOHAN H. LANGAARD

Director, Municipal Collections of Oslo

It has not yet been possible to determine the full scope of Edvard Munch's production. This much at least can be said with certainty: his production is enormous in comparison with that of most modern artists. At the time of his death he left no less than 1,008 paintings. To these must be added, besides drawings, watercolors, engravings and sculptures, all the paintings which the artist had given away or sold in the course of the good sixty years he wielded a brush.

A wide selection of Edvard Munch's works would scarcely fail to put his artistic quality into high relief. However, no exhibition can be large enough to throw light on all aspects of his captivating artistic personality. I am thinking now in particular of a certain characteristic feature in Munch, which he displayed already at the beginning of the nineties in the pictures forming the *Frieze of Life* series. I am thinking of the way in which it became apparently less important for him to produce single masterpieces than to find expression for whole series of ideas in large groups of ideologically connected pictures.

This is significant in more than one way. In the first place it tells us how he began at an early date to preoccupy himself with decorative problems. It was not because he wished to express any new primitivistic artistic feeling. It was because he perceived that he could only keep a large connected series of pictures assembled in one place by giving it the form of decorative wall-painting. He felt that he must be prepared to undertake a com-

mission of this nature if it were offered to him. An unkind fate prevented Edvard Munch from ever realizing the *Frieze of Life* in that way. The world had no room for the work in the special form he thought it required. In this respect it may be said that the artist's chief work from his youth was never carried out in full conformity with his real intentions. This is undoubtedly the greatest tragedy which has overtaken Norwegian art, although the individual pictures of the *Frieze of Life* can now and again be assembled and seen at one exhibition.

Munch did not allow himself to be affected or deterred by this ill fortune. When in 1907 he painted bathing life on the beach at Warnemünde, he still worked in the same way. He used the motif to compose three different pictures in such a way that they form the natural and clear symbol of an imaginative series of ideas. In their representation of unwakened youth, virile strength and elderly meditation, the pictures symbolize the everlasting character of the three ages.

In 1911 Edvard Munch won the competition for the privilege of decorating the new assembly hall of Oslo University, the so-called Aula. Thereby he gained his first and greatest chance of keeping a connected group of pictures united in the form of a large room decoration. Munch knew how to avail himself of this opportunity. He created the chief work of his maturity, and a work which raises the question whether his most beautiful artistic contribution is not found in the sphere of monumental wall decoration. Now that the artist is to be introduced seriously to the Anglo-Saxon public it must be made clear that he is in the same situation as so many great Italian masters of the Renaissance: much that is most excellent and most central in his enormous production can only be seen in the place where it was painted.

Munch, then, did not aim primarily at producing individual works of art, and this is no doubt one of the reasons why his pictures became so numerous that he could not possibly take adequate care of them. They were allowed to lie scattered about him inside and outside the house, in all kinds of weather and at all times of the year. Nevertheless, he would not dispense with them. It seemed as if his pictures served to retain the idea and thread in his thinking, and to remind him what his activity as a painter had taught him.

Munch entertained a constantly increasing reluctance to separate himself from anything he had painted. This had not always been avoidable. Until nearly 1909 he had lived under unusually pressing circumstances. Against his will he had often been forced to sell a picture belonging to one or other of his artistic series of ideas. In such cases he was apt to replace it immediately or later by a replica for his own use. The largest bathing picture from Warnemünde is such a replica.

This makeshift procedure afforded both advantages and disadvantages. It allowed Munch to leave behind an artistic collection which is probably unique in its completeness. This he bequeathed to the city of Oslo unconditionally, and Oslo will, at the earliest opportunity, build a museum for it. On the other hand it meant that a long time might elapse before the artist was able to paint his replicas. It was not possible for Munch to preserve these connected series of pictures in a form which, in both technical and formal respects, is entirely uniform.

No one perceived the drawbacks more clearly than Munch himself. In 1918 he examined his own example of the *Frieze of Life*. He thought that the work was too good to be forgotten. Nevertheless he compared it to a shipwrecked vessel which had had half its rigging washed overboard because it had not reached harbour in time. This comparison is the more apposite in that Munch's pictures have also suffered from the effects of weather by being allowed to lie about exposed to wind and rain. But an absolute catastrophe it has not been.

It is perhaps in the role of graphic artist that Munch has given fullest expression to his personality. Ever since 1894 he had made it almost a rule to expand his production through the mediums of etching, lithography and woodcut. This was not with a view to acquiring a reputation in a closely related field, but in order to fix his vision and his artistic ideas the more deeply and definitely. Munch's engravings have an independent value equal to anything else he has achieved. In their more than 714 different specimens they form a well-preserved, unbroken testimony of his activity as an artist.

But to return to this feature in Munch, that he did not aim chiefly at producing isolated works of art. It allows us to see an art which regards itself as a means of searching and plumbing the mystery of life and the universe. It is impossible to fail to see what this view of art at a certain period of Munch's life had taught him. The aforementioned bathing pictures from Warnemünde are particularly vivid illustrations. The lesson was not to allow himself to be absorbed by the sorrows and sufferings of the individual person at close quarters, but to observe how the great and lasting powers of Nature controlled life with rhythmic regularity. Munch aimed at freeing himself from an overpowering dread of life, which he had felt so intensely in his youth that it had threatened to crush him completely.

The result was an art which with unchanging intensity proclaims a view of life in constant growth— an art which gives its message as directly through its spirit as through its form. It is an art characterized by a certain visionary and imaginative romanticism. It may be that herein there is something typically Scandinavian which craves expression in the artist. If so, it has not limited Munch's universality. For all civilized adults, irrespective of sex, nationality and race, can read with equal facility the message Edvard Munch has tried to give them in his peculiar and deeply moving works.

22

22 SELF-PORTRAIT WITH A CIGARETTE 1895

Portrait of the Artist, taken late in life

Edvard Munch

Edvard Munch came of an old Norwegian family of considerable distinction. Grandfather and great-grandfather on his father's side had been church-men of importance. His father's older brother, Peter Andreas Munch, was Norway's great his-torian of the nineteenth century. The mother came of respectable farming and seafaring stock. Edvard himself is said to have been proud of his ancestry. One of the few, if not the only painting he made during his travels in Italy was of his uncle's grave in the Protestant cemetery in Rome. His bearing is described by those who knew him at various times during his long life as aristocratic, and he could have an extraordinary charm of manner. Physically he was a tall, striking figure. His noble head was imposing, well formed, with rounded brow, regular features and strong chin.

Munch was born at Engelhaug, a property near Løyten in southern Norway, on December 12, 1863. He was the second of five children. Soon after his birth the family moved to Christiania, the modern Oslo. When Munch was five his mother died of tuberculosis. Her place in the family was taken by her sister, Karen Bjølstad, a woman of great character and devotion. She lived until 1931 and it was to her and to his sister Inger that Munch addressed the letters that are the chief source of information about his life.[1] The aunt's letters to the nephew show her steadfast affection, and her wisdom and understanding at the most difficult times of his life. The very youthful journals that are published with the family letters give a picture of a normal family life. The father was a military doctor and he sometimes took the boy on visits to army posts, excursions which both enjoyed. Munch was often ill during childhood and poor health fre-quently interrupted his attendance at school. His interest in art appeared early. The total impression from the contemporary record then is of a frail, intelligent boy living with a closely knit, devoted family. The close family bonds were to hold throughout his life.

On the other hand, as Munch looked back on his childhood he was acutely conscious of its unhappy aspects. The mother's death was a heavier blow than appeared on the surface. Most serious for the family was the effect of this loss on the doctor father. He turned to religion with an intensity which appears to have made him indifferent to worldly success and which could be frightening to his children. In a conversation with his own physi-cian when he was an old man, Munch spoke of his early memories. The father 'had a difficult temper, inherited nervousness with periods of religious anxiety which could reach the borders of insanity as he paced back and forth in his room praying to God . . . When anxiety did not possess him, he could be like a child and joke and play with us . . . When he punished us . . . he could be almost in-sane in his violence . . . Disease and insanity were the black angels on guard at my cradle . . . In my childhood I felt always that I was treated in an unjust way, without a mother, sick, and with threatened punishment in Hell hanging over my head.'[2] When Edvard was fourteen his elder sister,

70 *Maiden and Death* 1894 Drypoint

76

76 *Summer Night* 1895 Drypoint and aquatint

Sophie, died of the same disease that had taken away his mother.

That these experiences of childhood made the deepest impression in the mind of a sensitive and introspective youth is shown not only by the artist's preoccupation with them at the end of his life, but also by the number of works of his early maturity whose subjects are taken from the family tragedies. Hopeless illness is the theme of *The Sick Child* of 1885–86. This painting Munch repeated six times in oils—the last repetitions are from the middle twenties (No. 57)—and twice in prints. The subject is, of course, his sister Sophie, and the 'mother' is the aunt. Scenes of Sophie's death are represented in two of the most striking paintings of the nineties, *The Death Chamber* of 1892, repeated in the lithograph of 1896 (page 25) and

By the Death Bed of 1895 (No. 18). In each scene the different members of the family are given characteristic poses. The father, bearded and bald, prays with clasped hands. The youngest daughter, Inger, who was the closest of the family to Edvard, looks toward the spectator, and her nervous hands and sensitive face betray an almost overpowering grief.

The last illness of mother and sister is certainly recalled by the painting *Spring* of 1889 in the National Gallery, Oslo. The frightening memory of the mother's death is the subject of the *Child and Dead Mother*, 1899, in the Bremen Kunsthalle. As late as 1902 the woodcut *Praying Man* reproduces another memory of childhood, of the father who had been dead fifteen years.

The artistic career of young Edvard began in his seventeenth year. Poor health had interrupted his formal schooling and appears to have ended his father's hope that he could become an engineer.

In any case, it was with his family's blessing that he entered the State School of Art and Handcraft in Oslo as a pupil of the academic sculptor Julius Middelthun. In 1882, at nineteen, Munch joined a group of young artists who set up a studio in a building where the leaders of the younger generation already had their ateliers. Foremost among them was Christian Krohg, eleven years Munch's senior, and it is he who is considered to have had the strongest influence on young Munch.

Krohg is an able representative of the international style of realism which spread from the art of Courbet and Manet in France. The author of the best German monograph on Munch, Glaser, compares Krohg to Uhde in Germany and Bastien-Le Page in France.[3] Americans might be struck by parallels with Winslow Homer, particularly in his paintings of seafaring subjects. The literalness in representing reality, the subdued color, and the emphasis on technical dexterity in manipulating paint which also mark Munch's work of the early eighties link him closely with Krohg. It is also a fact that the two men were friends; Krohg was one of the first to praise Munch's painting in print, and Munch was regarded by contemporaries as Krohg's pupil.

Munch himself, however, is quoted in every account of his life as saying that he owed more to another member of the older generation. This is the painter Heyerdahl, who is often more superficial than Krohg in his approach to subject matter, but who did possess a more brilliant technique. It is true that by the middle of the decade Munch had developed a free and very subtle handling of color. However, by this time he was approaching an attitude toward subject matter which was to lead him further and further from all his Norwegian contemporaries.

From the early eighties Munch's work showed qualities that were to persist or to continue to reappear in more developed forms. He assimilated ideas quickly and was dextrous with the brush. There is little awkwardness in the earliest works in which he follows the techniques of the older Norwegians. The paintings also show a sure sense of color that relies on limited combinations of tone for its effects. Far more significant for the later character of his art is the feeling that appears at the very start of his career for the relation of forms

to the emotional significance of his subjects. *The Hospital Ward* (No. 1) is ascribed to his eighteenth year and in this subject, which he knew from accompanying his father on his visits, he already has the ability to compose in a manner that concentrates on an expressive disposition of the forms. The theme is the lonely convalescent in the foreground opposed to the reclining patient with the visitor in the background. The right angle of the first figure is repeated in reverse by the pair of figures, establishing a relationship corresponding to the theme. It is surprising to realize that the device of figures in contrasting postures which Munch used so often in his later work is present in this painting which in subject and technique is typical of the naturalistic style of the time.

Difficult to define in its specific effects on Munch, but clearly very important in his early development, was the intellectual and aesthetic atmosphere which marked Oslo in the eighties. The political, social and moral controversies which occupied the whole western world in that period also affected Scandinavia and were particularly violent there in the spheres of moral and social issues. In Norway, no doubt because it had slept the deepest sleep of provincial isolation during the early nineteenth century, they were the most violent of all. In the Norwegian debates the most powerful voices were those of the two great literary figures of the second half of the century, Ibsen and Bjørnson, the former primarily on ethical and social questions and the latter in the sphere of liberal politics and the rising nationalism; and Munch's companions in the eighties took even more radical positions than these two veterans. The extreme of individualism, anarchism, with its ideas of the necessity of the abolition of the constraints of society and the state and its insistence on complete freedom for the individual, created the philosophical tone of the circle. In common with the foreign writer whom they most admired, Zola, they believed that the serious purpose of art was to provide a social weapon, a means of revealing the truth about life as it is, in the battle for freedom.

The particular battle in which blows were struck by Munch's friends was called by the Norwegians the 'Morality Dispute.' It centered on questions of sexual ethics and morals. The most forceful blow was the novel 'From Christiania's Bohemia' by the leader of the radicals in the group, Hans Jaeger. The title of the novel gave the name to the group by which they have been known ever since. It was published in December, 1885, and immediately suppressed. Jaeger was fined and actually served two sentences in prison as a punishment for publishing the book and for continuing to circulate it during the following year when there was great public excitement and controversy about it. The book is an autobiographical novel in which the sexual problems and experiences of the hero are described with extreme frankness. In the following year Christian Krohg, who had been a leader in the defense of Jaeger, published 'Albertine,' a novel of the life of a prostitute, where the inspiration of Zola seems evident. This book was likewise confiscated for indecency. In 1887 Krohg made one of his largest paintings of a scene from his novel, the inmates of the bordello in a police court. The canvas now hangs in the National Gallery of Oslo. Glaser states that there is a story that Munch painted one of the figures. This seems highly unlikely, but there is no doubt of his closeness to the leaders of Christiania's Bohemia. One result of this association on Munch's life was to mark him from his youth in the eyes of the public and particularly the conservative press as a member of a notorious and scandalous group.

The positive effect of the Bohemian experience was in his work. His companions provided subjects for paintings which are documents of the period. The outstanding portrait is that of Hans Jaeger, of 1889 (National Gallery, Oslo). Characteristic of the Bohemian motives is *Tête-à-Tête* (No. 4) which is called 'Paa Hybelen'—literally 'In the Den.' The Bohemian dandy, Jensen-Hjell, is recognized in the bearded man whose conversation seems to fascinate and perhaps shock a little the girl who looks at him across the table and through the tobacco smoke of a drinking place. The emphasis on the atmosphere and the psychological relationship recalls the method of the naturalistic novel of the time. Similar is the effect in the etching of 1895 which is, however, of the Christiania group of the eighties. Here Munch himself is the figure at the extreme left. The memories of these days lived on in Munch's mind just as did those of his childhood. In the 1920's Bohemian subjects reappear in painting and lithography, now treated with a detached and somewhat bitter irony. *The Bohemian's Death* of 1925 represents Jaeger who, dying of cancer, was brought from a nursing home to a hotel where his companions of twenty years ago could gather around him once more in the last few days of his life. This actually took place in 1910. The very last lithograph Munch made, a year before his own death, is a replica of an earlier print from the portrait of his friend painted more than fifty years before.

What must have been the most important examples of Munch's paintings as products of the Christiania Bohemia, *The Day After* and *Puberty*, are lost in their original versions of 1886, but each subject was painted again in 1894. The former (No. 14) is far closer in subject and treatment to the work of his contemporaries in the eighties. The carefully observed details tell the story—the dishevelled young woman with unbuttoned blouse, her posture on the bed of restless, intoxicated sleep, the empty bottles and used glasses on the table. The subject, of course, exactly accords with the themes of the novels of Jaeger and Krohg.

Puberty (No. 15) depends hardly at all on the method of detailed description. It is possible that the form was changed more radically in the later version than was the case with *The Day After*. Here again is the sexual problem, now seen much more subjectively, seen indeed as it exists in the mind of a young girl. Nevertheless, the basically realistic approach separates this painting, as well as its companion, from other paintings of the middle nineties. The atmosphere of the lonely bedroom, with the emphasis on the light and shadow from a single source—doubtless a candle—beyond the picture-frame to the left, and the realistic details in the anatomy of the adolescent figure describe the conditions that produce the girl's thoughts. The nature of these thoughts is revealed by the expression of the eyes, large and unfocused, the arms crossed in front of her body, and the hand unconsciously pressed between her knees. The fame of this painting rests on the way these things express a mingling of awareness, anticipation, and fear. Here Munch is obviously far more independent of established methods of procedure and the formulas of realism. Nevertheless, this probing into the beginnings of the consciousness of sex in an individual's life has a parallel in the autobiographical

revelations of Hans Jaeger's novel. Munch's concern with erotic and sexual problems which we see beginning in the eighties is even stronger in the next decade and, in spite of the changes he and his painting underwent, is a continuation of the early train of thought.

The change in his point of view toward the forms of painting, so pronounced in the nineties, also had its early beginnings. Following the direction we have seen in *Puberty*, there is greater and greater concentration on bringing out in an expressive and sometimes dramatic way the essential content of his subject. Munch subordinates all his means to this purpose. The development is not a straight and simple one, but the outstanding works of the middle eighties show Munch's growing strength in this direction. *The Sick Child* of 1885–86 is considered the finest example of his early work. Here, with very different means from those used in *Puberty*, there is a concentration on expression through the elimination of detail that Munch had not heretofore attempted. The opposition of the sick child's upright profile and the bowed head of the mother is the focus of the painting. Here the plasticity is concentrated, elsewhere the forms dissolve; and it is to this area where the accent is most of all on the child's head, that the color and composition direct the eye of the spectator.

The departure from the convention of solid, realistic painting brought adverse criticism when the painting was exhibited in 1886. According to an anecdote told by the painter himself his older contemporaries were by no means pleased. One of them said to him, 'I didn't think that was the kind of painting you were going to do.' 'Well,' Munch said he replied, 'everybody can't be painting nails and twigs.'

83 *Miss Ch. (The Nurse)* 1908 Drypoint

86

Even in the latest version of the painting in 1926 (No. 57) the basic character of the first is retained. The handling of the paint is in broader and freer strokes, and the paint is thinner. The accent on the girl's head is even stronger through the richness of the colors in that area. The very sensitive drawing of the original is more truly repeated, however, in the colored lithograph of 1896.

Many years later Munch published an account of painting the first version of *The Sick Child*.[4] To find a method of conveying his conception of the subject which he found expressed in the pale head of the model against the linen of the pillow, and in the trembling emotion of the mother, was a long struggle of painting and repainting. Finally he rubbed out the details of the setting which had detracted from the child's head and, as he put it, 'let everything stand in masses.' In the process of studying the model to find the solution he noticed that his own eyelashes affected the image, so he indicated it in the painting by a network of fine lines over the surface, apparently made with the pointed handle of a brush. It is characteristic of Munch that this evidence of the visual concentration that solved the problem was repeated in the version of 1926.

The theme of illness and the method of working from the model were both typical of the painting of his contemporaries. What was his own was his conception of the subject and the emphasis on form at the expense of literal realism. He accepted the limits of the prevailing naturalism of the time, by depending on what was actually before him in the model or the outdoor scene, but the procedure of concentrating his vision on forms that could convey the meaning he found in the subject, which he carried further than ever before in *The Sick Child*, was the basis of his work until the end of the eighties. The character of the form which is the vehicle of expression varies. A significant anticipation of Munch's work in the next decade in its motive and in its emphasis on lines and areas of tone is the painting *Inger on the Shore* of 1889.

The artistic horizon was widening in the late eighties and knowledge of French Impressionism was reaching Norway. A number of the older painters had studied in France. The leading figure in propagating French ideas was the painter Frits Thaulow. He was a man of means and in 1884 had offered to send young Munch to Paris for a few months as he had other young painters.[5] The offer was not accepted, but the next year Munch did go to that city for a visit of a few weeks. The free handling of the color of *The Sick Child* definitely suggests that he had some idea at that time of Impressionist methods. Several years later, in paintings of outdoor scenes, his approach to the vision and technique of the French school was much closer.

The composition of *The Evening Hour* (No. 5) and the manner in which it is painted are ultimately derived from the French, but Munch, with an emphasis that is less obvious than in *The Sick Child*, nevertheless revealed the particular meaning of the subject for him. The painting represents his sister Laura in a self-absorbed mood, unconscious of her surroundings—a landscape in soft evening light with small figures of a man and woman in the background. The spectator's eye is led into the space beyond her figure, but the isolation indicated by her posture and expression is reinforced by the composition. She is in the immediate foreground, the lower part of her body cut off by the frame, and the separation from the space beyond is emphasized by the accent of the verticals of the house directly behind her. In this painting of the melancholy sister Munch found a device which he employed in a number of later paintings to contrast the mood of an individual with that of nature.

II

By the end of the 1880's Munch's originality and importance as a painter were recognized by a small but important group which included his immediate contemporaries and older members of literary and artistic circles. He had exhibited since 1883 with the progressive group of Norwegian painters in their autumn exhibitions. Yet conservative critics and most of the press were unfavorable. In a material sense he had achieved very little success; the years toward the end of the eighties were difficult. In 1889, with the backing of two older painters, Frits Thaulow and Erik Werenskiøld, Munch applied for a Government stipend to permit him to study in Paris. In support of his application an exhibition of his work up to that year was held which is said to have been the first 'one-man show' given a

Norwegian artist. Munch won the grant, and, according to the established practice, it was renewed twice. From the autumn of 1889 to the summer of 1892, except for the intervening summers which he spent in Norway, Munch was abroad. He had been in Paris for a few weeks in 1885, but it was during this much longer period, under the full impact of the radical concepts of French painters, that decisive changes took place in his painting.

Although he was by no means unaware of Impressionism, then the major progressive tendency in Paris, in October of 1889 Munch entered the studio of the academic painter Léon Bonnat, whose prestige was at its height. He remained there as a student for three months. From his letters to his family we learn that Bonnat liked his drawing very much and that Munch expected to profit by what he was doing. However, it was impossible that the correct, academic realism of Bonnat could have given anything to Munch. Toward the end of his time with Bonnat, his father died very suddenly. Unable to reach home in time for the funeral, the son remained in Paris. By early January he had left Bonnat and moved from the city to St. Cloud where he was working independently.

The following year Munch became ill as soon as he arrived in France and he spent some weeks in a hospital at Le Havre. That winter he went to Nice for his health and returned to the Riviera again the next year. There was also a brief trip to Italy and one to Germany.

What Munch went through as a painter during these years was not simple. He followed diverse tendencies, some of which seem contradictory and were not, during this period at least, reconciled. Some led directly to the full artistic maturity of the nineties, others disappeared after a year or two to return later completely transformed. Thus this was a crucial period for Munch, supplying him with additional foundations for his painting that were to last until the end of his life. In this sense he can be compared with his French contemporaries, Bonnard and Vuillard, who also built on their experiences of the early nineties and, like Munch, absorbed only those innovations of the twentieth century which could be reconciled with the old bases of their art.

In the written sources so far published there is almost no information about the way Munch came to know the work of his contemporaries in Paris. The letters to his family show that his companions were Scandinavians. They contain references to visits to exhibitions, but no specific mention of paintings. Jens Thiis, who as an old friend was in a position to know, states that Munch knew the work of Vincent van Gogh and Gauguin at Théo van Gogh's gallery.[6]

Soon after he had left the studio of Bonnat, when he was in St. Cloud, he made an entry in his notebook which laid down what was to become the program for much of his later work. He wrote, 'No longer should you paint interiors with men reading and women knitting. There must be living beings who breathe and feel and love and suffer. I would paint such pictures in a cycle. People would understand the sacredness of them and take off their hats as if they were in church.'[7] The first sentence was a declaration of independence from the conventions of realistic genre painting, from which he had actually turned some years before. The idea of pictures in a cycle dealing with the living, loving and suffering of human beings expressed in such a way that the paintings strike awe in the beholder was the new challenge the painter presented himself, the culmination, no doubt, of feelings he had had from the period of creation of the first versions of *The Sick Child* and *Puberty*. The idea became Munch's *Frieze of Life*, whose scope in subject matter was not established until the end of the nineties, and whose limits were never clearly and finally defined. During this first Paris period only the first of the motives for the frieze were found. Until the end of his life Munch worked and reworked the motives of his cycle, always in the hope that he could find the opportunity to create it in one grand decorative scheme.

The thought expressed in the St. Cloud note-book represents only one pole of Munch's effort in these years. The opposite extreme was the product of his contact with the still-dominant current of progressive French painting, Impressionism. Munch devoted considerable time to paintings in this manner during 1890 and 1891, and with his facility with paint and his quick and impressionable mind he rapidly attained a grasp of the method of color and subtly balanced arrangement of pictorial elements. Adopting the Impressionist method completely meant taking a detached view of the relations and character of color and form in light. His impressionist paintings as a group are like a calm and untroubled island among his other works. It was in this manner that Munch won his first popular success. In 1891 the National Gallery of Norway made its first purchase from him, of an impressionistic view of Nice.

The point Munch finally reached in this direction is beyond the limits of the first generation of Impressionists and includes innovations of Seurat's Neo-Impressionism. The painting in which this extreme is most evident is the *Spring Day on the Karl Johan* of 1891 (No. 6). The handling and the relations of colors, particularly in the foreground figures, the vertical accents, the horizontal shadows and the long perspective lines seem echoes of Seurat's paintings. It is clear, however, that Munch was not interested in the most subtle and radical aspect of Seurat's art, the structural function of lines, shapes and colors in creating two-dimensional and three-dimensional effects. The Seurat-like features in Munch by no means dominate or control the canvas by their inter-relationships; rather, these borrowings supplied only a few of the elements of which the painting consists. The 'pointillist' manner of painting in uniform touches is not followed. The touch of the brush varies with the texture of objects, the color is broken or not, depending on the light, and the definiteness of contour likewise changes; basically, Munch is faithful to the older Impressionism. His pleasing and successful canvas comes very close to the best French work, but to that of an Impressionist painter influenced by Seurat, such as Pissarro.

Yet ultimately the importance of Seurat was great for Munch. After 1892 the impressionist manner was dropped, but even in the nineties his color shows the effect of Seurat's theories about complementaries. After 1900, when new tendencies appear in his painting, he returned to the problems of light and color and he came back to the application of the French painter's theories, but in a very different manner.

Impressionism for Munch at the beginning of the nineties was a temporary absorption in a kind of painting that had no relationship to the program he had announced for himself. But the brief movement in which a group of young Frenchmen participated under the leadership of Gauguin during the years Munch was in France did supply him with the means which he could apply to the problem of making pictures of the feeling, loving and suffering of living beings. Gauguin opposed Impressionism and Realism in order to create painting which could convey more than mere sensations. His method, which he called at various times symbolic or synthetic, involved reduction of modeling, elimination of gradations or division of tones, emphasis on contours and on linear relationships of a rhythmical character. He arrived at his relatively abstract forms subjectively and intuitively rather than by the precise calculation of Seurat. The goal and the method both have obvious affinities with Munch's character as an artist. His use of Gauguin's style is far different from his excursion in Impressionism. Instead of faithfully learning the principles of a new style like a student, Munch seized on the features of Gauguin which could be of immediate use to him. There was a complete assimilation to his own ends of the other's means. None of his works resemble Gauguin's or those of his younger followers as his impressionist paintings do their French models. There is no ground, however, for doubting the importance of Gauguin for Munch. The fact is that in 1891 unmistakable traces of Gauguin's style appear in paintings which mark a new departure for Munch. This is the very time when Gauguin had the strongest effect on his own countrymen. Furthermore, Munch continued to be interested during the nineties in the later ramifications of certain aspects of Gauguin's manner when, much transformed, they became a part of what is called 'Art Nouveau' or the 'Jugendstil.'

The paintings of 1891 which show this relationship to Gauguin are of subjects that became part of the *Frieze of Life*: *Man and Woman on the Shore*, formerly in Berlin, and the canvas called *Evening*, which has the additional title of *The Yellow Boat*. The latter was the canvas in which a new direction in Munch's style was first apparent. When Munch's paintings were exhibited in Oslo in the autumn of 1891 Christian Krohg published a very perceptive note on *Evening*.[8] He saw that it was an innovation for Munch, and for Norwegian art. 'When one has looked at it for a while and turns to the others, even to his [Munch's] own works, there is a gaping gulf between them,' and he recognized that the manipulation of lines and colors was 'related to

87

symbolism, the latest tendency in French art. The latest slogan is now resonant harmony in color. Has anyone heard such resonant colors as in this picture?' This musical, unrealistic quality struck Krohg the most and he also praised the yellow accent of the boat in the background which repeated the line of the horizon. He concluded, 'Thus we have the phenomenon that Munch, who here at home has been considered the most incorrigible of all the realists, the most impudent and reckless of all "ugly painters," is the first and only one to turn to idealism.'

The painting praised by Krohg can no longer be identified. There are three versions that correspond to the composition as he describes it, the shore line curving into the distance with a seated figure in the foreground, his head on his hand, looking over the calm water. All are dated 1895 or later, primarily because of their tonality and greater abstractness. A fourth version of the motive that seems earliest in style has the figure in the foreground in a different position, facing the spectator and cut off by the frame (No. 7). It was purchased by the owner, Christian Mustad, directly from Munch. The fact that this composition was not repeated in later versions in painting or woodcut, as the other composition was, may argue that this is actually Munch's first treatment of the theme. In any case, the Mustad painting has the characteristics described by Krohg, the areas of unbroken color, the curving shore line and the yellow boat which repeats the final line of the shore.

These are the traits of Gauguin's style; the meandering curves of the shore line in the foreground seem to be a specific echo. Unlike Gauguin is the deep recession of the lines into the distance. His Brittany paintings, which must have been Munch's ultimate source, have elimination of depth as an accompaniment of reduced modeling. It is by the movement back into space, however, that Munch makes the contrast of the moody figure in the foreground and the tranquillity of the shore, sea and sky of the Norwegian summer night.

Later, when Munch painted his *Frieze of Life*, he employed exclusively a manner of painting de-scended from the *Yellow Boat*, emphasizing in this later period its decorative and monumental possibilities. This, however, took place when the motives of the frieze had been found. During the next ten years his greatest effort was to find them, and the means he used in painting them differ according to the character of his motive. Subject matter has a predominant place in Munch's art and in this respect he differs basically from Gauguin and indeed from the painters who have led in Paris down to the present day. 'The concern with ideal qualities of art, that insistence on a world of ideal beauty and the conviction that this is realizable through art' which one of their best critics has said characterize French symbolist poets[9] were shared also by their contemporaries in painting. Nothing could be farther from Munch's method of procedure than that which Gauguin describes in explaining the genesis of his painting *Manoa Tupapau—The Spirit of the Dead Watches*: as he was painting the model, concentrating on harmony of lines and colors, a certain emotion seemed to be emerging from the picture which suggested the idea of the ghost beside the bed and provided the title.[10] Here the content follows the discovery of the form, and with Gauguin content in this sense is unprecise and vague—his 'inquiétude de mystère.' Munch's forms have significance when they are in a direct relation to his theme. His effort is not only to find forms, but images, pictorial ideas, motives which can convey what already is in his thought.

Even before 1891 Munch had been simplifying his forms for expression in a number of paintings which can be classified as distinct from the impressionist style or the Gauguin direction, although here the prevailing tendencies of French painting must also have played a role. Limited to a few colors or almost monochromatic, genre scenes are rendered with a new expressiveness of mood. Typical is the canvas *Night*, painted in blue and neutral tones, which represents a lonely man sitting by a window in the moonlight. The dramatic paintings of the gaming room at Monte Carlo belong to the same tendency. An early version of a motive for Munch's cycle painted in this manner, the *Kiss by the Window* of 1892 (No. 8), is still conceived realistically with strong emphasis on the window and the view into the street and the suggestion that the lovers have hidden themselves by the curtain.

87 *The Cry* 1895

93

The embrace suggested by the summary indications of posture and rendered in a silhouette is a concentration of expression through simplified means parallel to that of the *Yellow Boat*.

By the end of this early period abroad Munch had found his direction and possessed new means of

93 *Anxiety* 1896 In color

94 *The Urn* 1896

carrying it out. However, the uncertainties of attraction to opposed points of view had not disappeared. This is shown by the catalogue of the
exhibition he held in Oslo when he returned finally
from France. The titles reflect the phases he had
gone through. Along with the *Kiss*, *Evening* and
others of the new subject matter are titles which
belong to the point of view of art for art's sake—
Harmony in White and Blue, *Color-Mood in Blue*.
These last surprisingly resemble Whistler's titles.
It is possible that another phase of Munch's work
at this time may have been inspired by the American. The portrait of Inger Munch of 1892 (No. 9)
with its careful arrangement of tones restricted to
blue and black and a few warm accents brings his
work to mind. The consequence of this exhibition,
however, was to draw Munch into a new environment which was far removed from the atmosphere
of Parisian painting. Munch was invited by the
Union of Berlin Artists, on the initiative of the

Norwegian painter Adelsten Normann, to send his
pictures to its November exhibition. The showing
of his pictures in Berlin was a turning point in
Munch's career and also a significant event in the
history of art in Germany.

III

The exhibition in Berlin opened on Nov. 5, 1892,
and at once Munch's paintings became the center
of a bitter controversy. At a stage of taste where
Impressionism and the work of Manet were still
matters of debate Munch drew attacks as a disgrace
to art, and a demand was made within the Artists'
Union itself that the exhibition be closed. This
actually took place a week after the opening, over
the protest of a considerable minority of the members of the Union. This minority, under the leadership of Max Liebermann, the Impressionist, subsequently withdrew to found its own association,
the Berlin Secession, through whose exhibitions
the victory of Impressionism was won, and—

around the turn of the century—the first recognition achieved in Germany of the significance of the Post-Impressionist French painters.

Munch, urged by Normann, had come to Berlin with his pictures. Now he found himself the center of a battle between factions of German artists and a subject of discussion in the press. The whole affair seemed exciting and advantageous. He wrote to his aunt that 'all this uproar was great fun' and that there could not be better publicity. An art dealer approached him while the exhibition was still open with a proposal to exhibit the paintings in Düsseldorf and Cologne. Almost as soon as he had agreed Munch realized that he had made a mistake; an immediate independent exhibition in Berlin would have been more profitable. This Berlin exhibition did take place in January and admission receipts were good, but profits were low because of high expenses. Afterward the paintings went to Copenhagen, Breslau, Dresden and in June

to Munich. Munch stayed in Germany all this time, occupied with these exhibitions, making new friends in Berlin and painting vigorously.

This first long stay in Berlin was decisive for Munch. From 1892 until 1908, with returns to Norway in the summer and two winters in Paris, the greater part of his time was spent in Germany. From the beginning Munch found understanding critics and friends and finally important patrons and collectors of his art. Year after year he continued the campaign of exhibitions, with Copenhagen usually included with the German cities. The financial returns were irregular and meager during the first years in spite of the fact that his paintings were being shown continually. It was only after 1900 that a steady income from sales began. Munch never forgot that it was in Germany that he won recognition and success. He intended, until political events made him change, to acknowledge the debt by willing a painting to the

17

17 ANXIETY 1894

National Gallery of Berlin.[11] During the first years it was the hope of success and his stimulating circle of friends and companions that brought him back to Berlin after summers in Norway. He found his circle early. In January of the first winter he wrote his sister Inger, 'We Scandinavians, Strindberg, Gunnar Heiberg, Drachmann and I are almost continually together and meet in a little wine house.' This was the restaurant 'Zum Schwarzen Ferkel' which had been discovered by Strindberg and is well known to students of literature. Munch had joined a new Bohemia, more brilliant and sophisticated, but also more unstable than that of the earlier days in Oslo.

It was even more dominated by literary men and critics than the Norwegian group. There were German members as well as the Scandinavians Munch named, Dehmel, the poet, and the critic Meier-Graefe; but closest to Munch as a friend was the Polish poet and novelist Stanislas Przy-byszewski, who in 1893 married a young Norwegian, Dagny Juell, who was herself a remarkable person. It seems that Munch saw little of German painters.[12] Munch's new circle was part of the advance guard of literature, completely cognizant of what was going on in the rest of Europe. The intellectual environment was created by the ideas of writers with philosophic tendencies. Individuals held the various notions of the fin de siècle from the extreme of mysticism and occultism to the pessimism of deterministic science. Subjective and abstract thinking had taken the place of the simple old anarchism and realism of the Christiania Bohemia of the eighties.

96 *Separation* 1896

99 *The Death Chamber* 1896

The most obvious result of these Berlin years in Munch's painting was the concentration on subjects which were to be a part of his *Frieze of Life*. From 1892 to 1895 all but a few of the subjects associated with his cycle were established. However, the character of the themes had been set before Berlin: inner suffering of the individual in *The Yellow Boat*; the love of man and woman in *The Kiss* and *Man and Woman on the Shore*; finally death, for the earliest version of *The Death Chamber* is dated 1892 and was included in the first exhibition in Berlin. Each of these individual compositions was repeated in this period and the theme of each elaborated by new subjects, especially that of love. In the first exhibitions where the paintings were shown as belonging to a cycle, in 1894 and 1895, the canvases have the general title of 'Love.' This category continued the old Christiania-Bohemia concern with the sexual problem and it was also here that Munch had most in common with his literary friends in Berlin, particularly Strindberg and Przybyszewski. However, there is no need to assume that Munch was indebted for specific ideas to either. In the nineties he was far from the Strindberg of the deadly conflict of the sexes, and if he resembled him in his subjects at all it was in a few later paintings which reflected bitter personal experience. Munch's ideas, in fact, have parallels in literature from Baudelaire to the end of the century.

Although he was not systematic or always consistent, several broad conceptions can be felt underlying the subjects of Munch's work. The most basic involves the powerlessness of the individual before the great forces of nature—love and death. The people in his paintings seem under a spell as if they were possessed by something so completely that no power of individual will or decision remains. This may be desire for love as in the expression of longing in *Summer Night* (page 12), the attraction of the sexes for each other, in *The Kiss* and the prints called *Attraction*, or, in *Madonna* (No. 13), the ecstasy and pain of the act of love itself, and jealousy can likewise be in complete possession. The presence of death eliminates everything else from the mind in the scenes of the death of Sophie cited above. Then, with no specific cause, the presence of forces of nature themselves can fill the human being with fear and anxiety—

The Cry (No. 11) and *Anxiety* (No. 17). In each case the individual is in the grip of something beyond his control.

Also deterministic is a parallel idea of the unbridgeable gulf that separates the sexes. There are two obvious ways in which Munch sees this difference as it applies to woman. In one phase of her life, as an innocent maiden, she is unobtainable or unapproachable because she is self-absorbed in a world of her own dreams—*Separation* (page 24). With experience she becomes subject to the animal side of her nature, again a force beyond man's control which makes her both a danger to him and basically unobtainable by him. She can devour him as in *Vampire* (No. 12). Although in love, she can exist in a different world as in *Ashes* (No. 16) where the man is bowed in despondency while the woman stands as if in dream-like consciousness of her physical sensations (her meaning is made more explicit in the print of the same subject). In a series of paintings and prints, the first of which date from this Berlin period, Munch spelled out his conception. *Woman* is the title of these works (page 30), but in Norwegian it is usually *Woman in Three Stages*. The stages are innocence, experience or lasciviousness, and disillusionment or withdrawal from life; in each stage she is inaccessible to man. In the late version, that in the Rasmus Meyer Collection at Bergen from the end of the nineties, this last is made clear by the inclusion of the figure of a dejected male at the right. The theme was reworked again at the end of the nineties in the painting that is a summary of the love side of his frieze, the *Dance of Life* (No. 25).

Woman considered in herself, however, can be seen in an entirely different light. She is the creator of life in *Madonna*. Love for her can be death as *Maiden and Death* (page 11) seems to say, and she can suffer and inspire pity as in *Consolation*.

This bare outline of a view of life which can be deduced from Munch's work of the nineties serves to show that he shared the subjectivity and pessimism of that age. It also brings out the dilemma in his thought, the irresistible power of love and its inevitable consequence of pain or frustration, an indication of the troubled state of his own spirit. The themes of death, fear and anxiety point in the same direction. The systematic aspect of his ideas is less significant. He apparently never arrived in

130

130 *Self-Portrait Wearing a Hat* 1932

27

his own mind at a final determination on exactly what subjects belonged in the *Frieze of Life*. In the period of its genesis, Munch's effort was concentrated on making paintings that would convey his thought with the maximum impact and it was through the impact of the individual canvas that he made himself felt, not through notions that were commonplace in advanced literary circles.

In this effort to achieve impact Munch is anything but a purist. The motives themselves which embody the ideas are varied in type. There are childhood memories as sources for the death scenes. Others seem remote from actual experience and are analogous to literary description or figure of speech; for example, the vampire suggested by the possessive and lascivious embrace of a woman, or the vision of the episode of temptation in the mind of the jealous man (No. 19). Similar to uses in poetry is the symbol Munch makes of woman's hair. In a great majority of his works on the theme of the relation of male and female the woman's long tresses touch the man as if the power of her sex flowed through them. The nature of the contact corresponds to the degree and character of his subjection to her: this varies from *Vampire* where the woman's hair falls over the head and shoulders of the man and she is in complete possession to *Ashes* where only a few strands stream out toward him. At times an even more direct and obvious symbolism is resorted to. The woman of *Jealousy* reaches for an apple with Eve's gesture, or motives are added to the border of the main subject to make its meaning more explicit as in the lithograph of *Madonna* and in several portraits of the period. In a few instances traditional symbols are employed, the skeleton or the skull for death, or the heart for love. To the end of the nineties there are occasional uses of similar conventions in a manner that seems to reflect the late Romanticism of some German contemporaries, as in *The Urn*. There may also be borrowings from the Belgian, Rops.[13] But more important and characteristic of Munch's whole art are his own compositions of landscapes with figures which express the relation of the mood of nature to the human being. In the nineties the content of this type varies from the fear of *The Cry* to the compelling mood of the *Summer Night*.

When he had found his image Munch often painted it two or three times in a relatively short period. In some instances the process was one of clarifying and strengthening the composition (the versions of *The Death Chamber* are an example of this), but in other cases there are very slight differences among the versions of the same theme (*The Cry, Madonna, Jealousy*). The impression of Munch in the early nineties is of his being engaged in an intense search in many directions for means to convey his ideas and of his absorption in the solutions that strike him as right once he has found them.

Considered as a whole Munch's style of painting underwent simplification through his need for direct and clear-cut effects that would convey immediately the force of his idea. Munch tried to eliminate everything that did not contribute to one definite meaning. The steps in which the unessential details were left out for singleness of effect are illustrated by the stages of *The Kiss* from the early painting (No. 8) with its character of realistic genre, to the etching of 1895, and finally the last stage of the woodcut where the silhouette of the figures exists without any setting (page 42). Though never again as extreme as this, the works of the nineties were carried out with relatively few artistic means. Putting expression first, Munch looked solely for whatever methods most effectively conveyed the meaning of a particular theme.

This resulted in paintings of the same period often being very different in style. Some of the ways of handling the brush and color, characteristic of years before Berlin, survived, but for a new reason. Munch turned from manner to manner according to his need for a particular kind of expression. In the year 1894, for example, *Ashes* has broad areas of color with emphasis on shapes and contours, *Vampire* is freely brushed with a variety of strokes to establish forms in light and to create luminous shadows, while in *The Cry* the color, though painted flatly, is in systems of rhythmical lines and bands. This last example has been recognized as related to the contemporary decorative manner of the Jugendstil.[14]

Munch's method of arranging and relating the few forms and colors he depends on in each work was to avoid complexity or ambiguity by simple relationships. The repeated verticals of *Summer Night* and the surrounding shadow of *Vampire* emphasize the pose of the single figure and the compact group

105 *Lust* 1898

respectively. The clear opposition of vertical and horizontals of *Ashes* and the straight diagonal lines and the curves of *The Cry* are contrasts called for by the subjects.

Devices for treating or relating forms reappear in a number of paintings; Munch established a kind of vocabulary of expressive means. The single figure is often seen frontally to give a maximum effect of gesture and facial expression. To emphasize the difference in meaning of figures by the strongest accent on contrasting postures the opposition of front and profile view is repeated a number of times. The bowed man in profile and the woman frontal is the scheme of both *Ashes* and *Vampire*, different as they are in other respects. The foreground and background figures of *The Death Chamber* are disposed in the same way except for the half-turned figure of Munch himself which is the link between the two. Where relationship in

space is a factor, as it is here, the device of *The Yellow Boat* is used. The figures are large in scale in the immediate foreground with the movement into depth abrupt. In color Munch often makes use of predominantly somber tones with strong differences in light and dark for emphasis, and frequently depends on relations of complementaries or near-complementaries, reds or oranges against greens and purples, as the major contrast.

The need to express specific emotions led Munch to seek and in a number of instances to repeat representational motives capable of conveying a definite feeling or mood. There is a limited repertoire of these repeated motives which is analogous to his vocabulary of forms. The shore, sea and sky seen in so many paintings and prints—often recognizable as Aasgaardstrand, a village on the Oslo Fjord where Munch had spent summers since the late eighties—can play a specific emotional role. The space of the sea itself is communed with by Munch's absorbed and inaccessible maidens while before it his men are bowed. The character of the Norwegian summer gives the shore landscape a special meaning—as is felt in the flaming sunset of *The Cry*, the luminous sky and the diffused light of the summer night of *Attraction*, or the rising moon of *Summer Night* and *The Dance of Life*.

In representing the human figure Munch arrived at a few gestures and postures which he likewise repeated to impart a specific feeling. An obvious one is the bowed man for despondency. Johan Langaard has pointed to the motive of the woman with her arms held behind her as a formula for feminine provocativeness as she both holds herself back and offers herself.[15] It is the gesture of the women who wait in the moonlight, the Eve of *Jealousy* makes it as completely as she can, and it occurs in several portraits. A variation is *Madonna* where one arm is held behind her body while the other is raised to her head as if she offered and received simultaneously. The portrait of Madame Przybyszewski (No. 10) with her expression of irony and invitation, so far from the yearning of *Summer Night* and the other versions of the motive, shows that while Munch may have employed a formula it did not become a stereotype.

The four self-portraits Munch made at the end of this Berlin period are significant autobiographical documents. They illustrate, in the different ways in which the subject is conceived and rendered, the particular condition of Munch's art at this time. *In Hell* (No. 21) is freely brushed with a strong contrast of warm and cool colors and of light and shade, with the nude body modeled in yellows and oranges with green accents. *With a Cigarette* (No. 22) is almost monochromatic with its subdued

107 *Woman* 1899

112 *The Violin Concert* 1903

107

blues and purples except for the pale warm tones of the face and hand; the latter are painted solidly in fine strokes to build up modeling while the dark tones are brushed in thinly and sketchily. *Under the Mask* (No. 20) is painted flatly with a minimum of modeling. The image of himself burning in Hades is one of the themes which is like a figure of speech, and the placing of his own face beneath a woman's mask is a direct symbol as is the fragment of the skeleton in the lithograph self-portrait, the fourth of the decade (page 16). The portrait *With a Cigarette* has no overt symbol but depends on the representation of visual reality; it alone conveys a sense of a moment of real time and of natural atmosphere and space.

For all their differences each portrait has the same theme fundamentally, the inner tension and anxiety of the man, but each work presents a single aspect of the basic condition. They are all images of Munch as he thought of himself. He is suffering but bitterly defiant in the painting *In Hell.* In *Under the Mask* he seems absorbed in awareness of the woman's power and responds to it as the lowered lids and sensual, slightly parted lips make plain. The drawing in the lithograph of 1895 is very close to the latter, but the important difference is the shift of emphasis in the features: the lips are barely indicated while the eyes dominate with an expression of thought without the slightest hint of awareness of the senses. Under the spell of death, Munch is ascetic and somber; the black background, which eliminates the body and isolates the head, reinforces this other-worldly mood.

With a Cigarette presents Munch as he thought of himself as seen by the world. He stands slightly turned to the right, suggesting that he had been moving from left to right, his face turned toward the spectator as if his attention had been suddenly attracted, and pauses while the smoke of his cigarette rises. His eyes stare under arched brows, but

112

119

the sober cast of the features of the lower part of his face—the set chin and the lips in a straight line —seems due to serious thought. The hand holding the cigarette is tense with the outer fingers spread. The purplish shadow with which the coat and hair blend is cast by the single light-source of the painting. The figure emerges partially from the shadow just as the external distraction brings the mind from absorption in itself. This painting stands out from the other self-portraits in this relatively complex balance of inner and outer attention, and it differs from them correspondingly in the complexity of the way it is painted. Two things were required by Munch to convey his concept, luminous darks from which a few forms could stand out in light and precise articulation of the features and the hand; for each effect, as has been noted, he used paint in a different manner.

During the period of the first years in Berlin Munch achieved the position of an independent and mature artist. Uncertainties of direction no longer existed as they had in the years just past. The different styles in which he had then worked had been the result of his exploration of alternative possibilities in painting. Now many things had been dropped, Impressionism among them; and the diverse elements which remained had been subjected to a process of simplification. One expressive purpose was served throughout, even though in single paintings only a few elements of the diverse repertoire were used. Moreover, the few means of each painting were manipulated with the consistency and effectiveness of a mature painter.

This unity and consistency of Munch's art—the style of this phase of his career—is of an exceptional and, in fact, precarious order. His major effort, the paintings of the subjects of the *Frieze of Life*, have nothing of a frieze-like quality when looked at together. They differ in size, scale, degree of abstraction or of representation of nature, and in technique. They have in common the fact that their themes are related and that each is conveyed with the maximum visual impact possible, regardless of overall visual harmony.

Munch once wrote 'Art is crystallization';[16] these paintings seem crystallizations of his ideas of the fate of the individual man and woman in the grip of the forces of life and death. There is no parallel in the painting of his contemporaries to Munch's subordinating consistency of form and handling to communication of his ideas. Yet the concept of art as communication is an old idea which has an important place in the thought of the Romantic period, for example in Delacroix. Munch's extreme position means that he disregarded the two main concepts of the nature of form in painting on which the art of the second half of the nineteenth century rested. In the more important, such form and color are determined by the painter's relationship to the external world. Broken color in paint as the equivalent of pure visual experience in Impressionism, and the revolutionary structure of color and forms in Cézanne's painting derived from his subtle analysis of the relation of color to two- and three-dimensional effects in nature, are both products of this view. The other concept, often held concurrently with the first to a greater or less degree, considers that forms have inherent qualities and is concerned with revealing these by contrasts and harmonies among the forms themselves. This is the idealism which was becoming more pronounced in the French school toward the end of the century and on which we have touched in connection with Gauguin. In either case, the effort of the painter is to develop his means according to

119 *Omega and the Tiger* 1908–09

127 *Death of the Bohemian* 1927

127

33

logic and method, and we are accustomed to trace the evolution of a painter's style in terms of step-by-step changes in technique and in the way his forms are related, which correspond to the changes in his attitude toward nature or to the forms themselves. Munch does resemble his great French contemporaries in seeking to use forms in their most simple and unambiguous character. For this reason he can be in debt to the French school, and to Gauguin in particular; and can also be one of those who create new forms. But fundamentally he differs from them all, even from painters of imagination and fantasy like Odilon Redon and the Belgian Ensor who created a manner of painting calculated to convey the subjective character of their visions.

The precariousness of Munch's artistic position is in its dependence on a particular state of mind which was almost independent, in the last analysis, of the actual procedure of creating a picture, and, as time proved, was unable to survive as conditions in his own life changed. Although this attitude originated before the Berlin years, the powerful way it absorbed Munch there is evidence of the effect of the Berlin environment on him. Aspects of this phase continued to be important in his later work after more solid bases for his art had been found.

IV

In Berlin Munch won the recognition of the leaders of the intellectual and cultural life of that city. He established relationships that gave him devoted supporters and others which led ultimately to very substantial patronage. In these first years, however, the financial rewards were few. When success did come later it was first in the form of critical acclaim—'more honor than gold' as Munch used to write to his aunt. It was possibly disappointment at the small results of his strenuous efforts to win purchasers that led Munch to decide to go back to Paris. He had thought of this move in 1894 and he did go early in 1896. It is possible that Paris seemed more promising because of the interest that Scandinavian dramatists were creating there. In the letter of 1894 in which he speaks of Paris he relates that he has met Lugné Poë, the producer of Ibsen in that city.

Munch remained in Paris through all of 1896 and most of 1897. He exhibited his paintings twice in what must have been very favorable conditions, yet he appears to have had less material success than in Berlin; his work left only the faintest impression in France. His first exhibition was at Bing's gallery, 'L'Art Nouveau,' the second to be held at an establishment famous for giving its name to the well-known decorative style of the nineties. Strindberg wrote a poetic account of the paintings in 'La Revue Blanche.' In the following year Munch showed the subjects of his cycle again at the Salon des Indépendants. Gustave Coquiot, in his history of these salons and the artists who took part in them, makes the mere comment that 1897 was notable for the paintings of Douanier Rousseau and Signac. The few writings in French on Munch are more an indication of the curiosity and taste of individual Frenchmen than of any general awareness among writers or artists of Munch's significance.

That Munch was in touch with some of the leading figures in Paris is shown by the fact that he made a programme for 'Peer Gynt' for Poë's Théâtre de L'Œuvre and a lithograph portrait of Mallarmé. The pioneer dealer in advanced moderns, Vollard, included one print by Munch in one of his publications of modern print-makers, but no other important commercial house seems to have noticed Munch. Clovis Sagot, a minor buyer and seller of pictures, who appears later as one of the first to buy from the young Picasso, is said to have bought from Munch after the 1897 exhibition.

What little evidence Munch himself offers on the Paris period is in the few letters to his family that have been preserved and published. As before, many of his companions were Scandinavians. During the first part of 1896 Strindberg is mentioned, also the poet Obstfelder. He seems to have been intimate with the English composer Delius whom he may have known in Norway; for he not only mentions him in a letter of this time, but later when he returned to Paris for a short visit he stayed with him. Many years later when they were together in Wiesbaden he made several portraits of him in lithograph.

Munch's chief activity in Paris was as a graphic artist. In 1894 he had made his first prints, eight etchings and one lithograph, the initial essays in what was to become a most important part of his work. During the next year in Berlin the number of prints increased with a much larger proportion of lithographs. 1896 was one of the most productive years of his whole career.

The prints of the first years are especially close in subject to the paintings. The important works of the eighties as well as the new subjects of the early nineties were transposed into etching and lithography. The procedure of going over the same subject again and again was carried out now in prints; many themes exist in more than one graphic medium and Munch often took the pains to execute the plate or stone in reverse so that the print follows the disposition of the painting and is not a mirror image of it.

The styles that had been established in painting were carried over to the graphic works. Thus the diversity of the painting manners was continued in the prints. Yet Munch tried to exploit the special potentialities of each medium, and from the beginning made prints that can be considered as studies of this problem. Toward the end of the nineties the proportion of subjects repeated from painting grew less, but repetitions of paintings never entirely disappeared. At the same time Munch's works in each medium took on a more separate character. This was especially true of woodcut, the last technique that Munch attempted.

Munch's first prints were etchings in drypoint, a technique which he always favored and which he often combined with aquatint. Pure etching is less frequently employed. Munch handles the etcher's needle with great sensitiveness. This is particularly evident in the drypoint portraits where the flexibility of line possible in this technique permits delicate drawing and strong accents of dark. The hatched drypoint line gives the luminous darks necessary to recreate the atmosphere of the paintings of the eighties and early nineties. Aquatint gives the flat areas of tone which serve to recreate the broad areas of color in the paintings, as in *Summer Night*. Munch is more conventional in his etchings than in any other medium. He masters the established methods and applies them to the particular problems of his art, but aside from a few experiments with zincographs, some of which he printed from hand-colored plates, he does not succeed in finding new qualities. The extreme delicacy and complexity of modern etching methods no

doubt presented difficulties when it came to transposing bold effects and the simplified forms of his painting. Fewer subjects of the paintings appear in the etchings, and Munch used this medium less than the others. On the other hand, he favored etching for portraits.

Lithography was actually much better suited to the various manners of the paintings of the nineties. It invited broad handling, sweeping heavy or light lines, and made possible strong contrasts, since it could be used for the finest drawing or in heavy black washes. Further, it was suitable for work on a larger scale. Munch demonstrated the possibilities in his first series of lithographs in 1895. *The Cry* is executed in rhythmical systems of strong lines. *Madonna*, in the state of this year without color, has deep shadows, sweeping contours and light delicate modeling in the torso and face. The self-portrait also exploits the contrast of the washed-in black background and the light drawing of the head. Lithography as a method of reproducing a line-drawing appears also in this first year in a print that is interesting because its subject is of a type rare for Munch: *Tingel-Tangel* represents a Berlin music hall in a manner that recalls both Toulouse-Lautrec and Manet.

Munch's production of lithographs in Paris must have been encouraged and definitely was influenced technically by his relations with Auguste Clot. Clot has been called a genius for his skill as a printer. He is held to have been responsible for the interest in making colored prints on the part of Toulouse-Lautrec, Bonnard and Vuillard as well as for the technical perfection of their work. All of Munch's lithographs of 1896 were printed by Clot, and his first works in color, which are among them, were no doubt prepared in the shop of this expert printer, as was the practice of the French artists. In addition to the introduction to a new technique, the association with the Parisian printer must have brought Munch knowledge of the most advanced work in that city. In Munch's work from this Paris period and the years immediately following features appear which can be attributed to the influence of these young Frenchmen. But the great majority of the lithographs of 1896 show more independence. They have little relation to the French style, but rather continue the procedures of the year before.

Munch's nearest approach to a concern with the subtle effects of color of the French lithographs is in the print of *The Sick Child*, which is in four colors in its 1896 state. The repetition in color of the head of the child from the painting of ten years before demanded the most careful adjustment and interrelation of the tones. It is the finest technical achievement of this period. On the other hand, in the prints based on the paintings of the Berlin years, or those closely related to them, Munch's purpose was entirely different. Simplification of forms for direct expression was called for and in these prints Munch's methods are his own.

The colored lithograph of *Anxiety* (page 22) was the work of Munch chosen by Vollard for his album of modern prints. Here the color is confined to the red bands of cloud. This is in contrast to the landscape of vibrant black and white lines and the solid blacks and whites of the figures. The effects of the painting are conveyed in more reduced but very direct and vivid terms. This deliberate exploitation of the expressive advantages of the more limited graphic technique is characteristic of Munch's work in the nineties. The lithograph of *The Death Chamber*, also printed by Clot in 1896, is likewise a striking example. Printed without color, the solid blacks in a white setting are more abrupt and stark in their effect than the corresponding blues and tans of the painting. Both lithographs are thus further steps in simplification of means, a method of the period which has been noted in the versions of *The Kiss*. For Munch, graphic work of this type was not simply a means of reproducing a painting, but a way of continuing the thought that had reached its crystallization in the richer medium, as he might have put it himself.

Munch executed more prints in lithography than in either of the other graphic mediums. Its versatility is so great that in every phase of his later painting the problems raised could also be attacked in lithographs. The work in this medium therefore closely parallels the manners of painting. A print such as the *Violin Concert* (page 31) can be related to the paintings of the opening years of the new century when forms depend on closer observation of nature, yet it is the peculiarly graphic qualities that make it an outstanding work. The decorative balance of blacks and whites and the drawing of the figures which conveys the sense of the piano prelude coming to an end are very different from the forms of the earlier prints that have been discussed. But they are equally the products of Munch's understanding of lithography.

Even more important for Munch's art as a whole was the other graphic technique, the woodcut, in which he also began to work while he was in Paris. As with color lithography, new methods had been developed. There is evidence in the published letters that Munch knew Valloton's work when he was still in Berlin, but the powerful influence was from Gauguin who really created the modern woodcut. Gauguin's chief innovations became basic in Munch's own method—the emphasis on the quality of the surface of the wood in printing flat tones in broad areas (the ultimate source is the Japanese print) and on the character of the stroke of the knife or gouge which works the wood so as to produce varied and vibrant passages. One of his earliest woodcuts, a version of *Anxiety*, is particularly close to Gauguin in the way the light areas are treated. A further indication that Gauguin's work inspired Munch is in the fact that his first woodcuts are colored.

Woodcut had a unique place in Munch's art. From the beginning the technique interested him as such. The craftsman in Munch seems to have been challenged by a technique that was at the beginning of its development. Moreover, the woodcut with its expressive character held much the same significance for him as lithography. The difference in Munch's relation to the two techniques is that in woodcut he tends more and more to find forms in terms of the way the medium can best be worked, rather than forms drawn from painting. The result is the development of a technical originality and style with a consistency found nowhere else in his work. Munch's influence on artists of the Expressionist movement in Germany is most clearly seen in woodcut, for here he established a path that others could follow.

A good part of Munch's inventive ingenuity in woodcut was applied to making color prints, which he ultimately carried to a modern extreme of virtuosity. Early in his career as printmaker he found his own special method, which was to saw the woodblock in pieces after it had been cut, so that the parts could be inked and printed separately, although the whole composition had been worked

132 *Moonlight* 1896–1901 In color

out as one unit. He also printed from complete blocks in the usual way or combined the two methods. One experiment found in several early prints, notably in the later states of *The Kiss*, was to cut the figures out of the block so that they could be printed separately. Over this a second printing was made from a coarsely grained piece of pine lightly inked. The more usual method was to saw the block into two or more pieces along a contour in the scene represented, the shore line or the horizon. In many instances other blocks were made in addition; for example, *Woman's Head against the Shore* is printed from one block in two pieces and a second complete one. Almost twenty years later Munch took up again a number of the wood blocks of the end of the nineties and added new blocks for new colors. Here he attained his greatest virtuosity.

Two Beings, originally printed in two colors in 1899 from one block in two pieces, was later printed in combinations of four colors, and in the most complex state in seven, with a moon added and an overprinting of the details of the foreground rocks.

In the last few years of the century monochrome prints, usually black on white, became equally important with work in color. Although prints with forms similar to the paintings continued for a few years longer, Munch was moving away from the typical curving lines and rhythmical closed contours. In a few prints of 1899 a new position in regard to forms was clearly established. The dependence was on the simple contrast of the soft blacks of the inked wood and on cutting strokes made in the simplest way, long or short, often in groups parallel to each other. *The Old Fisherman* (page 44) is made on this very simple system. The vertical strokes of the background and the hat contrast with the shadows and with the twisted strokes which render the gnarled face, and the grain of the wood makes a series of fine white lines through the face and the lower part of the print which repeats in an abstract way the contrast of the heavier verticals above. The character of the wood and the character of the lines of the countenance are the major elements of the print.

The *Winter Landscape* of the same year has for its focus of expression the contrast of the tiny houses and the great expanse of dark in the sky and the white of the snow. Here the strokes are heavy, moving emphatically across the landscape and over the houses. The dwellings seem in the grip of the darkness and the deep snow of the northern winter. It is significant that these early examples of Munch's original method were his reaction to a specific experience of the external world. In his painting around the turn of the century a new concern for the experience of nature also begins to appear.

There are few paintings from his Paris period, but among them are studies of nudes carried out with a decorative emphasis on the contours and on the placing of the figure within the area of the canvas (No. 23). Their interest is that they reflect French painting—they seem closest to Bonnard. This direction may be explained by the fact that in Paris Munch was working on his first mural decoration, commissioned by Axel Heiberg, as he states in one of his letters.

Some major paintings of the last years of the century, done after Munch had left Paris, also depend on two-dimensional relations of clearly defined areas of color. One of the last important additions to his cycle is the *Dance of Life*, which in subject is a summary of the love side of the frieze. It is painted more flatly than any other painting of the series. The large areas of unbroken color, the lack of any expression of depth except for the diminution of the size of the background figures, give this painting a decorative and monumental character the earlier paintings lack. This quality and the motive of the figures against the background of the shore and sea reappeared when Munch received commissions for paintings for interior decoration. In this picture Munch found the solution to the problem of unity in the *Frieze of Life*.

Inheritance (No. 24), a new motive, for Munch at least, of pessimistic fatalism and social evils, like-wise follows a scheme of flat color and shallow space. This is also the character of the large *Mother and Daughter* of 1897 in the National Gallery in Oslo. These paintings show that Munch was becoming more aware of the problem of style as such, and that monumentality was the aspect of style on which his interest now centered. This latter quality, the result of forms ordered so that their effect can be perceived at a distance, became increasingly important for all of Munch's work, that intended for the decoration of walls and single paintings as well.

V

The first decade of the twentieth century brought great changes in Munch's position in the world, in his personal life, and in his art. From the last years of the nineties there was steady progress in financial success and in recognition of his importance as a painter. At the end of the decade he was secure economically and at last had achieved popular success in Norway. In his own life, on the contrary, this was a period of instability and increasing mental tension which came to a climax in the autumn of 1908 in what he himself called a complete nervous collapse.

The increasing importance to Munch of the experience of nature in the opening years of the century now set a trend. A new position was worked out in the years just following. After 1905 the changes accelerated until a high point of naturalism was reached in works around 1910. However, at the time of Munch's nervous crisis there were a number of works which seem, in subject matter at least, counter to the greater and greater emphasis on the objective world.

Until 1905, Norway was more the center of Munch's life and his painting than it had been since the eighties. Germany was important but the nature of his ties had changed; the old group of the early nineties had ceased to exist as such and more than previously Germany meant for him the place where he obtained commissions and sold his works.

The new direction in Munch's painting can be explained as a shift of emphasis in the process by which he arrived at the content and the form of his painting. Experience of the external world became a primary factor, the source of ideas and of images. Munch did not return to the realist or impressionist position of his youth: experience of nature is not a matter of visual sensations alone. Rather, he looked at the world to discover those universal forces of life that had preoccupied him. The nature of these forces was no longer sought through pure speculation on life, but through observation. If the basic aspects of Munch's thought continued, they were integrated in a new way with the functions of the painter as observer and creator of forms.

The methods of painting and the symbols of the nineties which directly contradicted actual experience now had to be eliminated. The 'overt symbols' and the extreme abstract forms such as were used in *The Cry* do not appear in painting after 1900, though they persist a little longer in prints which continue the motives of the nineties. In this Munch was following a general trend in painting which came after the extreme of symbolism. Only the devices which were in accord with real experience, especially those which expressed the relation of man and nature, could still be used. The variations of manner of painting and of the degree of abstractness or concreteness in representation diminished as the problem became that of expressing the universal meaning existing in a real world. As Munch's new position became established his technique changed in the direction of a more exact representation of visual reality.

In 1900 and 1901 Munch painted a group of landscapes that may be considered transitional since they continue the manner of painting which had come to the fore at the end of the nineties. Yet the flat areas of color and strongly emphasized contours are employed in a more complex way than in the landscape settings of the paintings of the nineties, or the closely related landscapes of that time. The greater elaboration of the forms and the greater concern for effects of light were required to render the subtle qualities of a specific scene, whereas earlier Munch had tended to reduce his means to the minimum. *The Island* (No. 29) contrasts the light sky and its reflection on the water with the dark shapes of island and shore. The play of the shapes of the trees in the foreground of *White Night* (No. 32) is even richer. The dark green of the trees with their blue shadows, the pale blue tones of snow and water and the blues and greens of the sky produce an effect of varied patterns and gradations of cool light of the winter night.

Girls on the Bridge (No. 30) re-uses an old motive, females absorbed in contemplation of the water in the quiet of the summer night. While the girls leaning against the railing recall the women standing on the shore gazing at the sea, there is now no special emphasis on posture or gesture to suggest anything specifically feminine in their action. On the contrary, they seem viewed as part of the larger harmony of the scene. Their white, red and green dresses, the strongest accents in the painting, contrast with the minor harmonies of lavender, neutralized blues, pinks and dark greens. The converging lines of the bridge carry the eye toward the girls and beyond to the shore, and the direction of the young women's gaze is at a right angle to this axis so that they are like a pivot in the composition. Foreground and background are further related by the reflection of the great trees in the water. The light is that of the northern summer night, evenly diffused from the luminous sky against which the shapes of the shore stand out sharply. The moon is setting, but itself gives no light. The integration of light, shape and space is more complete and subtle than in *The Island* or *Winter Night*.

The scene was one which Munch knew well and to which he returned for motives of other pictures. The 'bridge' is the pier to the dock at Aasgaardstrand, which still retains its old form though now it is concrete and iron, and the house behind the garden wall and the two great lindens with their single silhouette are today as they were at the beginning of the century. This harmony of areas of color and rhythmical contours, primarily verticals, horizontals and diagonals with curves in a secondary role, is the last phase of the manner of painting which began with the *Yellow Boat* and here the musical quality of that painting has its richest expression.

The most radical departure from anything he had done before was the painting *Melancholia* (No. 28). 1900 is the date assigned in recent literature, and in spite of the difference in use of forms and colors, this is undoubtedly correct. There are points in common with works done that year and near it in the flat areas of color and the convention of the curving outlines of the pattern in the cover of the table and of the tree seen through the window. The subject of this powerful painting is the abnormal state of the model. The distortion of the spatial

171

171 Wood Block for *Two Beings*

133 *In the Man's Brain* 1897

effects expresses her isolation from all awareness of her surroundings as she becomes locked in her own disordered thoughts. She sits in a brightly lighted room, her back to the windows and her dark clothes opposed to the warm colors and the clear light around her. The tile floor at the right and the table top at the left are seen from a different angle of vision from that of the rest of the objects in the painting: they are tipped up toward the spectator as if he were standing very close and looked down to see them. The curve of the table moves back into space beyond the figure and toward the window through which the fjord and its distant horizon are seen. The French door on the right, however, reinforces the effect of shallow space of the tipped-up perspective by the angle of the line along its base.

Moreover, the edge of the door continues the vertical of the subject's arm and the line of the corner of the room rises from the center of the top of her head, emphasizing her immobility and canceling any effect of recession in the corner. It is evident that Munch thought of warm colors as coming forward and cool as receding, for the door is painted in oranges and yellows while through the window the view is all greens and grey-blues. The woman seems confined in space, hemmed in between the table and the corner, but the spectator, aided by the arrow-like pattern of the table cloth, is aware of what she is not, the other direction in the painting, from the flowers on the far edge of the table to the window and out into the space of the world beyond.

The new elements that make this painting different from Munch's contemporary works are due to the influence of Van Gogh. The color may give a hint of this source, but the chief thing that Munch took

34

34 BOYS, GIRLS AND DUCKS 1903

from the Dutch painter was a method of distorting space effects for expression. The idea of manipulating the space by combining two angles of vision in one picture must have come from some such painting as Van Gogh's *Zouave Milliet*. Its use by Munch was very different, however, and was in fact more complicated. It is significant that similar distortions in this middle period of his work were used by Munch when the subject, as it did here, had a particularly personal meaning.

Far more typical was Munch's method of selecting aspects of reality as subjects for paintings where he could feel the embodiment of something more significant than mere appearances. The symbolism was implied discretely in what could pass for a representation of everyday life if Munch had not emphasized the things which point to a specific idea, as the flowers, the pine tree and the distant shore do in the painting just discussed. One of the last new subjects of the *Frieze of Life*, another representation of the theme of death, is a painting of a funeral procession in the Leipziger Platz in

Berlin of the year 1902, which, superficially at least, is simply an ordinary scene of the city. In the same year, 1902, the ages of human life is the subject of two paintings, one in the Rasmus Meyer Collection and the other in Stockholm, of a little girl, her mother and two older women in a village street. Langaard is no doubt correct in his suggestion that the charming *Four Little Girls of Aasgaardstrand* (No. 33) was painted by Munch as a complement to his 1903 portrait group of the four little sons of his patron, Max Linde of Lübeck. In this sense the Aasgaardstrand painting is the necessary opposite of the German portrait, but Munch hints at distinctions between the girls themselves which recall his ideas about women. The qualities of childhood in the little girls, from the ages of about three to eight, naturally come first in emphasis. Nevertheless, the oldest child who is at the left stands straight with her hands at her sides and takes the pose of Munch's woman who withdraws from life, while the prettiest of the four, in her red hat, with auburn hair and rosy cheeks, stands in

136

the familiar pose of the woman with her arms held behind her back.

Munch painted a number of pictures of children in the early years of the century and usually his interest was in the characteristics of the stage of life as such. An amusing emphasis on little boys as opposed to girls is the representation of going home from school in the painting *Boys, Girls and Ducks* (No. 34). The aggressive boys are in a compact mass behind their leader in the foreground, while the girls form a quiet and withdrawn group under the tree.

A new, freer manner of painting appeared in Munch's works of 1904. The flat tones are replaced by color applied in varied brush strokes in a number of tones, although not in the high-keyed palette of Impressionism. *The Garden Wall* (No. 35), another view of the great trees of Aasgaardstrand, is painted in a way meant to bring out the differences of the textures and the surfaces of the earth and rocks in the foreground, the smooth surface of the wall and the foliage of the trees. Paintings of the following years carry this direction further, but for one kind of work Munch continued the old, more abstract style. This was in paintings intended for the decoration of a specific place. Munch received two such commissions, the first in 1904 from Linde of Lübeck, who rejected the pictures when they had been completed, and the other in 1906 from Max Reinhardt for his theatre in Berlin. It is probable that the *People on the Beach* (No. 36), since it is approximately of the dimensions of the paintings of the Linde Frieze (as they are called) and is similar to them in subject, was painted as a study

for this project. The juxtaposition of the men and women on the shore without differentiation of their feelings or any expression of interaction between the sexes is another evidence of the change in Munch from the previous decade.

In the years 1905 to 1908 Munch emphasized more and more the rendering of actual visual experience in his painting. At the same time symbolic content was stressed more strongly. *Adam and Eve* (No. 37), which represents a young woman and a young man in an orchard, is painted in vibrant broken colors with a verve and a freedom that is a return to Impressionism, and yet the concentration of the man on the woman, as she stands apparently unaware of him and about to bite an apple, establishes the note of sexual tension. In Munch's version of the story, the man is the one who feels temptation. Preoccupation with themes of the relations of the sexes increased in 1906 and 1907. There can be no doubt that this was a reflection of his own increasing inner tension.

136 *The Kiss (Fourth State)* 1897–1902

140 *Winter Landscape* 1898

142

142 *Old Fisherman* 1899

147 *Girl's Head Against the Shore* 1899
In color

Munch attributed his troubles to a series of un-happy experiences in the years 1902 and 1904.[17] In his own view the deepest wound was the climax in the former year of a troubled love affair which had begun three or four years earlier. Discretion is still maintained concerning this relationship. The woman has never been named in print, but it is stated that she was the daughter of a wealthy Norwegian family. The first reference in Munch's published correspondence in 1899 shows that at that time he was trying to free himself, although she insisted on marriage, which struck him as ridiculous. After that, information is scanty, but the story of the bizarre conclusion of the affair has been told many times. A hoax was planned—Munch in later references usually blamed the woman and her Bohemian friends—by which she laid herself out as if on her death bed in order to bring him to her once more. Subsequently, in another attempt to hold him, she threatened to shoot herself and Munch

was shot in a finger of his left hand when he tried to restrain her. In the final separation a financial settlement on Munch's part was required. The reason for this is not known, but the obligation lasted for a number of years. The payment of what he called 'blood money' to a person who did not need it was particularly odious.

Munch's disturbance over these events seems to have been slight at the time. He wrote from Berlin in March 1902 that he was getting over the economic blow and he added, 'as to the physical shock she has given me, I have completely recovered from that.' Later in the year he mentioned the wounded finger several times in ways that indicate deeper physical as well as psychic distress. From 1903 on references to his nervous state appeared in his letters. This condition may account for and certainly was increased by the other public scandals in which he became involved.

A contributing factor in all of these episodes was

150

very probably immoderate drinking, but to account for Munch's actions it must also be assumed that he was in an overwrought and over-sensitive state where his response to real or imagined injury was violent. In 1902 at Aasgaardstrand, as the result of a quarrel that had elements of a brawl, Munch beat a man named Ditten. A more public scandal was a fight which ended in the arrest of both parties in a café in Copenhagen in 1904. The papers of that city played up the affair as disgraceful behavior of Bohemians and there was discussion in the Norwegian press as to who was to blame. In 1905 at Aasgaardstrand Munch quarreled with the gifted young Norwegian painter Ludvig Karsten, whose portrait, now in the Thiel Gallery at Stockholm, he must have just finished painting. Again the powerful Munch was the victor, but now the aftermath must have been too much for him, for he left Norway during summer of that year, not to return until 1909. Because he could not face people whom he con-

sidered hostile—and judging from his letters he linked critics of his work with his other 'enemies'—Munch had avoided Oslo since 1904. Now he exiled himself entirely. Fortunately his paintings were having more and more success in Germany. His first major patron had been Max Linde of Lübeck. Then for several years Weimar became the center of his life abroad. Munch had first visited that city in the winter of 1904 through Count Harry Kessler, whom he had known in the early days in Berlin and who is best known outside Germany as the patron of the sculptor Maillol. Now that he was in real difficulties his Weimar friends, Kessler and especially Frau Förster-Nietzsche, the sister of the philosopher, were important supports for him.

150 *Man and Woman* 1899 In color

154 *Old Man Praying* 1902 In color

154

47

People and the city upset him, and in 1905 he stayed for a time at Bad Elgersburg in the neighborhood of Weimar; the following year he took a cure at Bad Kosen in Thuringia, on the advice of his friends. Yet during all this time he was busy painting. More commissions arrived for portraits than he cared to accept; he painted for the Esche family in Chemnitz and he had commissions in Hamburg. In 1906 Max Reinhardt ordered a series of paintings for a room in his Berlin Kammerspielhaus and sketches for a production of Ibsen's 'Ghosts.' At the same time the Swedish banker, Ernest Thiel, was making his collection of Munchs.

In the summer of 1907 Munch went to the village of Warnemünde on the Baltic which charmed him because it reminded him of Aasgaardstrand. He stayed for over a year except for the winter months of 1907–08. At the end of the summer of 1908 it appears that he determined to return to Norway. Later he stated that he had been in the best health in years at Warnemünde, but in Copenhagen, in the company of an obscure writer, he went on a four-day drinking spree. His troubles then returned more strongly than ever and he entered the clinic of a psychiatrist, Professor Jacobson.

Munch stayed in the Copenhagen sanitarium eight months undergoing treatment which included rest, baths, and most important of all, no doubt, complete elimination of alcohol; he drank very little during the rest of his life. During this period he wrote to his family and sent many letters to his friend Jappe Nilssen;[18] painted, made lithographs of animals in the Copenhagen zoo, and did the series *Alpha and Omega*. He was also occupied arranging exhibitions in Oslo and Bergen and with the sale of his pictures.

While Munch was under treatment his success in the world continued—in fact it reached the highest point yet attained. He wrote that he had made more money than ever from the sale of prints and paintings. Honors came as well as gold. In the autumn of 1908 he was made a knight of the Norwegian order of St. Olaf, an honor Munch said he might have refused if circumstances had been different. As it was, the arrival of the decoration caused a pleasing stir among the nurses. The next spring his old friend Jens Thiis became director of the National Gallery and at once began purchasing important early Munchs in Germany and negotiating

with Munch himself for others. It was also in 1909 that Olaf Schou made his first and largest gift of Munch paintings to the National Gallery, so that the majority of what is today the most imposing group of his works on permanent exhibition belonged to the nation at this early date. Rasmus Meyer of Bergen was forming his collection which he was to leave to his city. Furthermore, Munch's exhibition in Oslo was a popular success. When he returned to Norway in the late spring of 1909 major victories had been won.

Many of the paintings of the last years in Germany reflect Munch's struggle within himself, most plainly in his return to themes of love. In 1905 there was a self-portrait in the embrace of a woman and this motive was repeated in the painting and woodcut of the heads of a man and woman kissing, in one of which Munch's features can be recognized in the tortured face of the man (page 50). New subjects such as *Amor and Psyche* appeared in 1906 and 1907 and old ones were repeated, *Jealousy* and *Consolation*, for example, now in the new manner of color and atmosphere.

The most bitter work on woman, which like the self-portraits must have been the result of his persistent brooding over his own experience, is now known as *Marat's Death* (No. 39). Here the extreme of the idea of the defeat of the male is reached. He lies murdered while the woman stands erect and rigid, pressing her arms against her sides, excluding every feeling but that of her own self-justification expressed by the frozen and obsessive determination on her face. The focus of expression is the woman. The traits of her physical femininity are in contrast to the massive physique of the dead man; the juxtaposition of his powerful hand and hers is a telling detail. Light falls on her nude body, modeling its forms softly in pale tones of lavender, yellow and pink which oppose the strongly brushed, rich colors of the table and still life, the bed and the corpse. The other relations of forms are to emphasize her upright, stiff pose. Her body is the perpendicular of a right-angled triangle formed with the body of the man. The distortion of space brought about by the device of the shifting angle of vision used in *Melancholia* has the same effect. She is seen as directly opposite the observer, frontally, whereas the table, man and bed are viewed more from above. Her verticality is in contrast to and is independent of everything else. The red-haired nude of this savage picture should be compared with two earlier nudes, one in a painting of 1900 (No. 26), the other in a colored lithograph of 1901, both of which represent different forms of feminine self-obsession, possibly self-pity in the painting and sensuality in the print. It is probably right that these are three views of the woman whom Munch considered the chief source of his ills.

Munch called the self-portrait painted in Weimar in 1906 a self-examination. The intensity of his worried state appears in the agitation of his features—pursed lips, one eyebrow raised while the gaze seems fixed. The forms of the painting are designed to concentrate the spectator's attention on these features and secondarily to represent the subject's lonely isolation in the almost empty restaurant. Again the position from which the view is taken establishes the expressive relations of the forms in a single focus. The vanishing-point of the perspective is behind the head with the spectator's position close to the foreground; the lines of the tables converge sharply, emphasizing the figure's closeness and leading the eye to the face. The distance of the background is diminished by the dull red square on the green wall which frames the head. In fact the play of reds and greens in the figure as opposed to the violet and orange of the tables and the shadows—an insistent repetition of near-complementaries—seems to be calculated to produce an effect of agitation in accord with that of the features.

Munch's inner discomfort may very well have been a compelling reason for the very pronounced efforts he made during these years to affirm values in experience outside himself. His increasing emphasis on rendering effects of light and texture is particularly evident in a series of paintings of nudes of 1906 and 1907.

There is considerable difference in the way Munch studies these nudes. Those of 1906 are seen quite objectively in the setting of the bedroom. Others, in the following year, although in several cases painted in the same setting, stress the mood of the model, which is conveyed by her bowed head. The motive seems to be an extreme of feminine shyness, and perhaps an older, non-professional model gave the suggestion. With either type of nude, however, Munch was concerned with what he saw and felt in his model, not with himself.

During his year at Warnemünde Munch succeeded in going beyond these studies and established a new and affirmative position in his conception of subject as well. His main effort was in paintings of the motive of bathing men (Nos. 43–45). Bathers had been subjects for Munch before but in the sense of the everyday life of the seashore. His Warnemünde bathers are in the form of a triptych, at the left a youth, in the center mature men and at the right an old man. The subject of the ages of man is analogous to the theme of the paintings of women of six years before, but the genre character of everyday life is gone and the emphasis is on the virile dignity of the nude bathers. The composition of horizontals and verticals and the controlled but vigorous movement of the men of the central canvas, as Langaard has pointed out, create a balance in the painting.[19] The painting is in broad areas of colors, complementary yellows and lavenders, and browns and purples, to give the effect of brilliant sunlight. Another kind of balance is in the relation of the figures to this brilliant nature: these men stand self-sufficient in their own strength, a rejection of the dominance of humans by nature's moods of the earlier periods. Munch attached importance to this work. He wished it hung in the most prominent place in the Oslo exhibition of 1909 and when the original triptych had been sold he painted again the central and left panels, for which, apparently, no complete study had been made.

A second motive found at Warnemünde was not developed as completely at that time, although it was one which became important to Munch later. This is the working man as a subject. Later we know Munch regarded workers as the most important social force of his time. Now he represents them in his manner of picturing ordinary experience while characteristically stressing the types—the mechanic in his dark clothes and the mason in white (No. 42).

One of Munch's works made while he was in the Copenhagen sanitarium can be looked on as another and significant step in the process of mastering himself, the series of eighteen lithographs telling a parable, under the title of *Alpha and Omega*, of man and woman, but now 'in fun and earnest', as Munch wrote himself. The first idea came while he was at Warnemünde in a series of drawings of

155

155 *Man and Woman Kissing* 1904

the first humans.[20] The significant thing as it was carried out in lithography is that, though the pessimistic theme is the familiar one for Munch, it can be approached with sufficient detachment to permit a note of ironic self-ridicule. The story is simple: Alpha is the man and Omega the woman; the scene is a terrestrial paradise. After the first happiness, the woman directs her unsatisfied love to the animals—in earlier lithographs Munch had caricatured his rivals and 'enemies' as animals. The irony and the pathos lie in Alpha's ridiculous efforts to recapture her affections. His efforts are bound to fail and he cannot understand why. Omega is obeying nature and when she embraces the animals and kisses flowers she is more a part of the forces of life than the man can ever be. In the end, though he slays the faithless woman, he in turn is killed by

her progeny, the monstrous children begotten by the beasts.

Munch made two major paintings at this time, the self-portrait in the Rasmus Meyer Collection and the portrait of his doctor, Professor Jacobson (No. 46). Portraiture, of which he had done much since 1900, was of course one type of work in which objectivity was a necessity. It is evident that Munch looked at his psychiatrist with at least as sharp an eye as that with which the patient was regarded. In a rich painting of warm reds and browns and purples the doctor is rendered as full of suppressed excitement, alert and voluble, but intelligent, a type very far from that of the detached and patient scientist. Jacobson has been characterized by one who remembers him as a strange man in whom there was the scientist, the artist and, perhaps, something of the poseur.

When he returned to Norway and was living at Kragerø, Munch painted portraits of the friends who had stood by him so loyally when they came to visit him, and those of Jappe Nilssen, Jens Thiis, and Thorvald Stang (No. 47) are outstanding. He also painted the rocky coast and the sea, the Norwegian nature to which he had so often referred with longing when he wrote from abroad. These Kragerø landscapes of 1910–12 are the most faithful, straightforward studies of nature of Munch's mature career (No. 48).

VI

The return to Norway in 1909 began a new mode of life for Munch. From the first years at Kragerø, to the final period which lasted almost thirty years when Ekely on the outskirts of Oslo was his home, the external aspects of his life remained the same. He lived alone and usually avoided people. He was not a recluse, however, as the portraits of his friends and the many personal reminiscences published after his death testify. He rarely saw members of his own family, but he kept in close touch with them by letter as he had always done, and provided for their support more generously now that his own income was ample.

As time went on, Munch became more and more indifferent about selling his paintings, and the demand from Germany and Scandinavia grew, so that no effort on his part was needed. Ultimately it became difficult to purchase directly from the artist. It is said that he did promote the sale of his prints and that this was an important source of income, especially during the twenties. This is borne out by the number of later printings and new states of his early works. Though his relations with the outside world were limited in these different ways, Munch retained his fondness for travel. He continued to go to Germany and Denmark during the years before 1914, and during the twenties he was in Germany a number of times and also visited Paris and Italy.

The changes in Munch's existence did not mean a transformation of the man himself. He was not freed from inner disquiet, for he told his physician, probably when he was in his seventies, 'The last part of my life has been an effort to stand up. My path has always been along an abyss.'[21] By avoiding the shocks he feared he was able to maintain a life devoted to his work. Furthermore, this work shows that he actually had attained a poise that permitted

the carrying forward of his ideas with a broader view of life and a clearer penetration into the problems of his own art.

During the first years after his return to Norway Munch painted largely within the framework of his ideas of the years immediately before, but he broadened their implications. The theme of the workmen, for example, was continued in a series of paintings of snow-shovelers in which the casual, accidental character of the Warnemünde treatment of the subject is entirely gone and a dignified and monumental effect not unlike that of the *Bathing Men* is achieved. In a version of 1911 the vigorous forward movement of the central canvas of the triptych is applied to the shovelers who stride toward the spectator through high piles of snow.

In 1910 Munch accepted an invitation to enter the competition for the decoration of the auditorium in a new wing that had been built at the University at Oslo. The difficulties that he had in winning the final award after the jury had selected his project by a two-to-one vote was the last evidence of real opposition to his art in Norway. The final decision did not come until 1914. Preliminary studies for the decorative scheme were also developed from earlier work. The large canvas called *Life*, formerly in the Dresden Gallery but now the property of the City of Oslo and soon to be installed in the new city hall, is considered to be such a study. The composition is a combination of a number of motives and ideas that had been used before by Munch, but there is also a new element. Grouped under a tree in summer dresses are women who represent the types of their sex. Near them is a despondent young man, related to similar figures of the nineties; opposite him an old man, detached from the others and looking up to the sky, is the most emphasized figure in the composition. This new element, old age as wisdom, can be seen as the further development of a motive of the *Bathing Men*. Another early idea for the murals was a composition of humans striving up a mountain toward the sun, which, similarly, is the further development of an idea of the painting of the bathers. The old man as wisdom and the power of the sun are two of the major motives in the University murals as they were finally carried out.

In the final solution Munch combined two themes. One is mankind and the forces of nature. The sun

160

rising from the sea framed by the rocks of the shore fills the wall behind the stage on the main axis of the room (No. 50). On adjacent panels are nude men and women, awakened by the sun and turning toward its warmth. Other panels with nudes continue the idea of man in harmony with other of nature's forces. The second theme, a broad conception of education, occupies the main panels of the two long walls. History is symbolized by an old man seated beneath a great oak with the Kragerø shore in the background, telling a story to a little boy. Opposite, the painting called *Alma Mater* is of a mother nursing a child with other children beside her who explore the life of the sea shore. The mode of each painting is that of the symbol in everyday life, though in these canvases the monumental replaces the casual. On the other hand, the nudes symbolizing man and nature belong to a type of invention more related to the *Frieze of Life*.

Munch emphasized the connection between the two cycles. In a pamphlet printed for an exhibition of the frieze paintings in 1918 he wrote, 'The Frieze of Life should also be seen in connection with the University decorations, for which it was in many respects a forerunner. . . . They should be seen together as ideas. The Frieze of Life is the joys and sorrows of the individual human seen close, the University decorations are the great eternal forces.'[22] The University paintings are also a culmination of Munch's efforts to establish values independent of his own state of mind, which took definite form in the years 1907 and 1908.

In the decoration of the walls of this public building Munch, who, with the exception of the series of mural paintings for special clients, heretofore had worked at making easel pictures where the content was the result of a personal evaluation of experience, now turned to the task of reaching a broad public. The formal language is simple and uncomplicated to achieve both clarity and dignity. The symbolism and the allegory are clear to the point of being familiar, for Munch ran the risk, in order to address an unsophisticated public, of using motives close to established popular visual tradition. Moreover, the paintings have his sincere feel-

ing for the look of his native land and the vigor and hope of its life, emotions shared by the mass of his fellow countrymen. This may be one of the reasons the murals are so highly valued by Norwegians. In any case, that Munch could have held and expressed emotions felt by everyone—and this, of course, is not restricted to the University paintings —accounts for the fact that in the parts of the world that know his work he is loved and esteemed by masses of people as is no other modern painter except Van Gogh.

In 1912 Munch received a different kind of recognition in Germany at the Cologne Sonderbund Exhibition. This was intended to be a survey of the contemporary movement in painting and also a presentation in individual retrospective exhibitions of works of painters who had special significance for the movement as a whole. This comprehensive undertaking was the inspiration for the New York Armory Show of 1913. Munch and Picasso were given galleries to themselves as important living artists. The chief emphasis went to Van Gogh and there were also separate showings of Cézanne, Gauguin, and to represent Neo-Impressionism, H. E. Cross and Signac. Critical opinion since agrees with this contemporary estimate of Munch's historical significance, and he is regarded as one of the important sources of the German movement of Expressionism.

Munch's relation to Expressionism was as a forerunner who established attitudes and a direction of thought. As the Cologne exhibition demonstrated, Van Gogh had the largest significance for modern painting in the minds of the Germans themselves, and the Frenchmen of the end of the nineteenth century were of great importance. In comparison to these, Munch's contribution to the movement, with the exception of the technique of woodcut, was confined to a conception of art. Only occasionally are the motives or the forms of the early Expressionists traceable to Munch; in both respects the others gave the Germans much more. In portraiture, where the attitude of the painter toward his subject was a determining factor in the character of the form, the Germans' work does recall Munch.

By 1912 the differences between Munch and these younger contemporaries had become great both because of the direction of his own painting and

160 *Self-Portrait* 1911

because of that the German movement had taken. The Expressionists had taken part in the innovations of the twentieth century, often carrying to extremes elements of Post-Impressionism which had not themselves affected Munch. There was also a strong tendency among the Germans to carry the aspects of their thought that had affinity to Munch's into radically new phases. The inner forces of the world were seen in the most elemental way possible, often as something all-pervading, relatively undifferentiated, and no longer necessarily linked to a specific human situation or emotion. Furthermore, they were interested in primitive arts, those of the natives of Africa and Oceania, and in the forms of the late medieval woodcut, preoccupations of the twentieth century that did not touch Munch. The drastic and systematic distortions and the abrupt opposition of strong colors which give many Expressionist paintings their quality of intense animation were very unlike his work. He had accompanied his paintings to Cologne. There he was pleased and surprised at the emphasis given him, and he was struck by the difference between himself and the new generation. 'Here the wildest things in Europe are collected— I am quite faded and classic,' he wrote his friend Jappe Nilssen.

Munch remained independent of contemporary art for the rest of his career, but not through indifference to what was being done, for there is evidence that he was interested in new work, for example, that of Paul Klee.[23] The problems that occupied him at the time of the Cologne exhibition derived from his own past work, but soon it was apparent that Munch's approach to these problems was changing. His purposes were not altered, but the different sides of his art were seen more in terms of the special problems and possibilities of each. Questions of technique and form became more prominent. Old subject matter continued to absorb him in connection with projects for wall decorations, but in easel paintings the method of finding a specific idea in the images of everyday experience was largely given up.

A major preoccupation in the last decades of his life was to carry out his original intention for the *Frieze of Life*, to make it a true frieze that would be suitable for installation in a public place where the impact of the cycle as a whole could be felt. When he purchased the property of Ekely in Skøien, just outside of Oslo, one of his reasons was to have space in order to work on large canvases. He constructed open-air studios, courtyards surrounded by high walls with narrow roofs just sufficient to keep the worst of the weather off his canvases. Here Munch could work out of doors in winter and summer. He was occupied not only with paintings for the frieze, but also with the University murals. The large painting of *Alma Mater* in particular had not satisfied him when the paintings were installed and he continued to work on it for many years. There are now actually two canvases of *Alma Mater* on the wall of the University, one mounted over the other. It is likely that Munch never came to a final solution. The other cycle, although he worked on it up to the end of his life, remained as studies in various stages of completion, for the opportunity to carry out the frieze in its entirety never came. Toward the end of his life another mural project was undertaken and likewise never completed. At the end of the twenties Munch was invited to take part in the decoration of the Oslo City Hall that was then being planned. The studies for a composition based on the motive of workmen for the City Hall are placed in the middle thirties. The war stopped all work of this sort in Norway. The number of paintings related to all of the mural cycles in his studio at the time of his death testify to the important place they occupied in the last period of Munch's life.

Munch had one opportunity, no doubt on a more limited scale than he wished, to carry out a decorative series where he could use themes from the *Frieze of Life*. In 1922 he executed twelve canvases for the large employees' dining room of the Freia chocolate factory in Oslo. Motives from the frieze of young people on the shore and from the Aasgaardstrand paintings of 1902 to 1905 together with other scenes of life in the fishing village provide the subjects. The style is sketchy and free, with the chief emphasis given to areas of color rather than to the contours and lines of the early works. The series has an informality and freshness that is appropriate to the uses of the room and its unpretentious modern style of decoration. The Freia paintings may give no idea of what Munch would have done had the chance come to paint the frieze as a whole, but they show his ability to adapt his ideas and style to a specific decorative problem and carry it out with verve and charm.

Consciousness of the possibilities of his techniques in relation to the different phases of his thought is characteristic of Munch's later work in general. It accounts for the increasing difference between works connected with his mural schemes and the easel paintings which were ends in themselves. Certain kinds of subjects became almost entirely confined to his graphic mediums. This had been true earlier when caricatures were done in lithography alone. During the years between 1910 and 1920 erotic themes of the kind that formerly had been treated in painting were confined largely to lithographs and etchings as if they had a private character more suited to the graphic medium. In woodcut there was also a return to the old themes. In the years around 1920 when he became interested in illustrating Ibsen, he used woodcut for the series from 'The Pretenders.'

When Munch went back to woodcut after his return to Norway—he had made none during the years 1906 to 1910—most of the work during the first years was dependent on the style of his paintings. The self-portrait of 1911 (page 52) is conceived as three-dimensional form revealed by light. The strong opposition possible in woodcut, rather than the nature of the material, is exploited. The lights bring out the features powerfully and contrast with the dark shadows of the eye-sockets to create the character in the portrait. The light vertical lines at the left, while they do follow the grain of the wood, count as lights that let the outline of the head appear and give the impression of the bulk of the head.

Within the next few years Munch took up old woodcut problems when he returned to the subjects of the early prints and to the old blocks to make new states in more complex color. A print such as the *Sun Bather* of 1915 is a transposition into colored woodcut of the effects of nudes in sunlight seen in the paintings of bathers of the middle 'teens, but the technique of woodcut produces results far removed from representation. The abstractly expressive character of the technique reaches its peak in one of the early prints of the series from Ibsen's 'The Pretenders,' *The Last Hour*. The staccato whites and blacks which render the courtyard and the figures standing in the back-

ground create an environment that seems to quiver around the prominent figure of King Skule, a contrast that—though very different in means—recalls the relation of figures and background in the painting *Anxiety* of many years before. Munch's representation does not correspond exactly to any precise moment of the action of the play, but it conveys the dramatic tenseness of the scene near the close when Skule, pursued by his enemies and having taken refuge in a nunnery, waits for the sanctuary to be violated and for his own death.

Munch's versatility in woodcut is brought out in a print of the same series which is dated late in the twenties. *The Trial by Fire* is the opening scene of the play. By undergoing the ordeal Inga establishes the legitimacy of Haakon, Skule's rival. In this print the accent is on the figure of Inga, who shows her unblemished hands to the witnesses. The delicacy of modeling and drawing expresses the character of the woman who has submitted to the barbarous test for the sake of her son.

Very closely related to the figure of Inga are three woodcuts of one of Munch's favorite models done late in his life. They are interesting because they continue the thought in the representation of the character from Ibsen: woman is portrayed as possessing the inner strength and the devotion required for self-sacrifice. The version known as *Birgitte III* (page 57) is the most sensitive expression of these qualities. This mature conception is expressed by a subtle use of the woodcut in which the styles of his earlier manners are integrated. The grain of the wood prints vertical white lines through the darks. The light areas of the face and neck are made by scratching away the surface of the block in vertical strokes. Light pervades the print and flows over the features which are suffused with feeling, yet the consciousness of the grain of the wood and the cutting of the block consistent with it are never lost. This integration of expressive representation with the abstract qualities inherent in making the print from wood is the final stage of what Munch began in the woodcuts of the end of the nineties.

The main direction of Munch's easel painting was toward an analogous integration of means. The change in his outlook at the beginning of the century had turned him from the methods of the nineties. After his return to Norway there were

169

further modifications of the arbitrary procedures that had been retained. Munch now demanded that his painting accord with a more consistent way of seeing nature. Distortions such as multiple angles of vision which had been employed so effectively could no longer be used, nor could obviously deliberate geometrical arrangements such as the contrast of horizontals and verticals of the *Bathing Men*.[24] Yet within the limits of this more natural visual logic Munch searched for expression as intently as ever. One of the solutions he found in the period from 1910 to 1920 involved further development of the figure or group of figures moving forward in space. This pictorial idea begins at the end of the eighties when Munch was interested in Impressionism, and he had employed it many times since. At Warnemünde it had been given a new form in the central canvas of the *Bathing Men* which had been repeated in the *Snow Shovelers*. The *Galloping Horse* of 1912 (No. 49) is based on a new conception of the idea. The setting recedes in a sharp perspective, with rapid diminution in scale of the objects in it, and the horse, vigorously foreshortened, head thrust forward, seems to bound forward out of the receding space of the picture. This exuberant expression of sheer animal motion and vitality is reinforced by the contrast of the warm browns and oranges of his coat against the whites of the snow. The painting is the climax of the Kragerø works which display a joy in the physical sensation of nature hitherto rare in Munch.

Three years later in *Workmen Coming Home* (No. 51) a similar method is used. The perspective now is long and deep and out of it the workmen

170

march. They are coming toward the spectator and also seem to be passing by him through the surface of the painting, an effect produced by the position from which the scene is viewed; the figure at the right which is cut off by the frame is seen from the side and from above. The advancing movement is accentuated by the thrust-forward head and shoulders of this figure, an effect even more pronounced in the second workman, whose face is a focal point in the painting. The upper parts of the figures in the foreground have a bulk which gives the movement weight and adds to its power. A lithograph repeats this composition but with the addition of a top-hatted figure at the left who turns to stare as the workmen go past, showing that Munch had a specific idea about the working man when he conceived the painting.

This painting, and the *Galloping Horse*, bring to mind effects produced by the motion picture. The movement seems to continue beyond the surface of the canvas and the foreshortening is exaggerated; so that the horse's legs, and the legs of the second workman, appear to recede beneath the forward-moving body. A film made by photographing a moving object with a camera mounted on a vehicle in front of it and moving at the same speed produces the sense of a setting flying back while the object moves forward and suggests the distortions in foreshortening of the *Galloping Horse*. The other painting may be compared to motion pictures of street scenes where people go past a stationary camera.

It would be entirely in character for Munch, who was always quick to seize a device or an idea that suited his needs, to have been impressed by the spatial images of the new pictorial medium of that day. There are other paintings of the period that seem to bear out this hypothesis. A replica of the workmen painting of 1919 in the Copenhagen Museum, however, lacks the distortions of the earlier picture. Whether or not Munch was influenced by the motion picture, his interest was now turning away from the problem of strong movement in space.

Space was a matter of major concern in the landscapes of the twenties, but its character was determined by the manner in which stationary objects were perceived. Animation of the space was still an aim, but the methods used to attain it were often the opposite of those used in the paintings just discussed. Instead of relations worked out from one focal point, a more natural vision which perceives near objects in relation to far objects was the basis. This was not a return to the abrupt shifts in the angle of vision of the paintings of 1900 and 1906; rather the aim was to create a continuous effect of space, which occasionally also recalls that of Van Gogh.

The *Landscape with a Starry Sky* of 1923 (No. 56) is the view from the porch of his house at Ekely. The railings of the steps and the shadow are large in scale as if seen very close, a demarcation of the immediate foreground which serves to project the eye into space. From this the movement goes back through a series of expanding arcs to the final distance of the horizon beyond the lights. The strong and somber accents in the foreground and the pale blue and green winter sky create a dramatic mood that is very characteristic of Munch. This quality, and perhaps a remark of Munch's, has supplied a literary title. The landscape is sometimes called 'John Gabriel Borkman' because the wood in the painting suggests the setting of the last act of Ibsen's play, the snowy hillside with the wood where Borkman died.

In paintings in the twenties, where the stress is on the exploitation of sensations of color and texture as at no earlier time, associations with specific ideas still persist. There is a series of paintings of a model in the nude in different poses done in the middle of the decade where the canvases have titles of the times of day. There is almost nothing in the way they are painted to justify this, although there is evidence that they were intended to be seen together. Munch's habits of thought invited titles for pictures and it is said that he welcomed suggestions from his friends. In paintings of nudes Munch, with a few possible exceptions in his work before 1907, never is interested in painting externals as if a nude were simply another motive on the same level as other things that the eye sees. To a greater or a less degree the emphasis is on the emotions of the subject. *The Nude* of 1926 (No. 59) is the extreme case where the inner sensitivity of the woman is stressed. This quality has invoked a title, *The Gothic Girl*, which, incidentally, is also attached to other females painted at this time. At the other end of the scale is the *Model on the Sofa*

55

55 ON THE VERANDAH 1923

(No. 58), rich in the painting of color and reflected lights where the physical and the external dominate, but where the revelation of a mood peculiarly feminine is not entirely lacking.

The *Nude by the Armchair* (No. 60), painted in the last year of the decade, is the final and richest stage of the interest in sensuous effects of color and light. The bowed head gives the hint of the self-consciousness of a girl, which insures that the spectator feels her existence as a living and feeling being. Indeed the theme of the painting is the relation of the living flesh of the model to the room and its inanimate objects, a motive which was begun in the nudes of 1907 in which the model likewise has her head bowed. The delicate play of reflected lights on the nude body—from cool to warm tones above and the reverse below the waist where the influence of the reds of the chair is felt—is opposed to the more definite tones of the objects and the room itself. The drama is in the sensations themselves and the composition is contrived to bring it out. The nude fills the canvas from top to bottom and is turned slightly, so that as the eye explores the space of the picture it moves from the surface of her body to the richly colored chair and into the space beyond.

The growing maturity of Munch's mind that underlies the whole development of his painting in the period of his life after his return to Norway manifests itself in still another fashion, in a detached view of himself and of his own past. In the self-portrait *Spanish Influenza* of 1919 (No. 53) he regards himself externally, and finds the convalescent in the first phase of recovery from an illness. The emphasis is on purely visual factors; the position of the robed figure in the space and the light is a pictorial problem solved by the relations of the areas of tone. The traces of his illness, however, are objectively observed in the features—red nostrils, blurred eyes and breathing through the open mouth. In the twenties self-portraits continue the objectivity with stronger emphasis on surface effects. At the same time he painted and executed in lithography recalled subjects of the old Bohemian days and of Hans Jaeger's death.

As he grew older Munch thought increasingly about his past. During the thirties the letters from his sister Inger contain many references to their childhood which must have interested him. Munch occupied himself at this time going over his early works. It is possible that this activity suggested the paintings of the middle thirties dealing with episodes in his life during the last days of Aasgaardstrand in 1905.[25]

The two canvases he completed—there were three in all but the third does not involve Munch himself—are concerned with the episode of his fight with the painter Karsten, who had died almost ten years before. There is an etching of this which is supposed, probably correctly, to have been made shortly after the event. The contestants are both sprawled on the ground making a half-apologetic joke of what must have been anything but humorous. A painting after the etching belongs to the years around 1916, to judge by its style. When he returned to the subject after seventy, it appeared in an entirely new light (No. 62). With complete seriousness he considered the shocking brutality of the assault. It is the passion and the force in the event, not himself as personally guilty or blameless, that is emphasized. The intensity of the aggressive power in Munch's black figure is brought out by a concentration on its bulk and expressive movement that is like Daumier. The passage where the curve of the back leads to the thrust-forward head while the shoulders are pulled back so that the arms are ready to strike reveals the plasticity and the action of the body with a simplicity of means that parallels the method of the nineteenth-century master. Facing him is his opponent in the white summer clothes of the Stockholm portrait, bleeding and frightened. His figure, in the rendering of its form and its articulation—feet wide apart and arm rigidly in the plane of the thin body—produces exactly the opposite effect, lack of bulk and impossibility of coordinated action. To this drama of contrasts so characteristic of Munch's late work is added the shock of the action in the quiet village street.

A companion painting, *Unwelcome Guests* (No. 61) represents what in all probability took place after the fight. The drunken hallucination and the impulse to kill are presented with the same detachment, free from any associations of personal emotion. Both paintings are conceived as if actors were now playing the roles which he himself had created long ago with such painful results. The figure in the foreground is very close to the corresponding figure in the fight painting and Munch uses the same technical means: outlines in crayon and broadly brushed paint. The image of Karsten at the window has the same gesture as in the other painting, but is even more unsubstantial. Add the naturalness of the spatial setting to these close similarities, and to the fact that it is difficult to believe that Munch could have seen himself so objectively at the time of the event, and we are forced to the conclusion that the paintings both belong to the same date. In publications since Munch's death *Unwelcome Guests* has been dated 1905. But it had not been published during Munch's lifetime. Indeed, the repetition of the figure of Karsten in the attitude of his helplessness might be taken as an indication that it was begun after *The Fight* had been completed.

The self-portraits of the last decade show characteristic habits of mind continuing to the end. Now, no more than earlier, did Munch attempt to express a multiplicity of meanings in a single image. His method was the opposite of the use of nuance and complex associations required for this kind of painting. Syntheses of ideas in Munch could occur only by combinations of images each of which carries its own meaning—the *Dance of Life* is a typical example. When Munch was preoccupied with a theme he approached it in different ways and 'crystallized' each finding in an image. This method persisted from the beginning of his work, though his evaluation of life and experience was continually evolving. Now in his old age he regarded himself from different points of view as he had in the nineties and at other periods of his life. But his view of himself is more often external, and when he embodied what are purely ideas about himself in paint the terms were those true to visual experience.

A characteristic of his later life is represented in the painting called *Nocturnal Wanderer* where the old man, suffering from insomnia, his eyes dark from lack of sleep, walks about the empty house. The frugality of his life is the subject of the *Cod Lunch*, where he is eating what must be a most humble Norwegian dish, boiled codfish head. In another painting he caricatured himself as a wizened old man—he was in fact robust-looking to the end and had few of the marked traits of age—standing behind a table full of bottles, an attribute of his youth.

It may be supposed that this fantasy of himself in the role that was disastrous for him many years before is connected with the current of thought of the *Unwelcome Guests*. An ironic note may be intended in the contrast between what he feels himself to be and what he was.

Thoughts of age and accompanying ironic self-examination are a theme of another late painting, *Between the Clock and the Bed* (No. 63). The caricatured old man, a little ridiculous in his posture, is in the same kind of brightly colored surroundings in which he posed his models a decade before. Now the opposition is between this world of visual sensation and the old man who appears to be unaware of it, standing as if concentrating all his attention on hearing the tick of the clock. There is no note of pathos in this freshly painted picture which so obviously contradicts the theme as it applies to himself.

In contrast to this painting built around an idea is the self-portrait which is held to be the last he painted (No. 64). The conception is straightforward and direct, Munch as he saw himself in the light of day as he really was. The setting is very simple and a clear light falls on the figure. The modeling is in broadly applied tones that establish the bulk of the figure and the more closely defined planes of the massive bony structure of the head. The strength in his age that was surprising to himself and to his sister is in the deep chest, broad shoulders and the easy, negligent carriage. The expression of the face is conveyed by the eyes, which are steady beneath the heavy lids, and the lines of the face which suggest his age. The lips turn down, but are firmly set. The strength which carried him through life and the traces of his vulnerability to it are both present.

Munch died while Norway was occupied by the Germans. Long before the invasion his relations with Germany had been altered by the Nazis. In 1933 on his seventieth birthday Munch had received congratulations from all over Europe. In 1935 his work was included in the Nazi exhibition of degenerate art in Munich and in 1939 fourteen paintings and over fifty graphic works from public collections in Germany were sold by the German Government at auction in Oslo. During the occupation the letters to his sister show them helping each other meet the difficulties of war-time restrictions.

Munch was worried about the safety of his paintings, a matter that he could not cope with himself, old as he was and living alone.

A little more than a month after his eightieth birthday, on January 23, 1944, he died of a heart attack. His will, after providing for his sister and his niece, left all his works to the city of Oslo and the residue of his estate to be disposed of at the discretion of the court.[26] The large number of paintings, prints and drawings left by Munch are stored in the studio at Ekely, awaiting installation in a new municipal museum in Oslo which is being planned. The classifying and cataloguing of this material and the editing of Munch's notebooks and letters are under way. When the devoted Norwegians who are responsible for these undertakings complete their task the world will have a new and more complete understanding of their great countryman.

158 *Old Men and Boys* 1904

Notes to the Text

1   Bibliography 112 passim. References are made here-after to the family letters only when this source is not named in the text

2   Bibl. 6, pp. 17, 18

3   Bibl. 21, p. 14

4   Bibl. 107

5   Bibl. 112, p. 56

6   Bibl. 91, p. 26

7   Bibl. 108

8   Bibl. 46, pp. 193, 194

9   C. M. Bowra, *The Heritage of Symbolism*, London, 1943, p. 6

10 See Robert M. Goldwater, 'The Genesis of a Picture.' *Critique*, I, 1946, pp. 5 ff.

11 Bibl. 4, p. 4

12 Hermann Schlittgen the caricaturist is the only German artist mentioned in the family letters. Bibl. 112, p. 127

13 Iconography was not the only thing borrowed. The composition of *Madonna* is derived from Franz von Stuck. Bibl. 9. Rops had long been known to Munch; *Puberty* recalls Rops' lithograph *Le Dernier Amour de Don Juan*

14 Ernst Michalski, 'Die Entwicklungsgeschichtliche Bedeutung des Jugendstils.' *Repertorium für Kunstwissenschaft*, 46, 1925, p. 148

15 Bibl. 54

16 Bibl. 108

17 Bibl. 5, pp. 31–38

18 These letters (Bibl. 5) are the chief source of information for the events immediately before and the period in Copenhagen

19 Bibl. 54, p. 56. It has also been observed that the pose of the figures of the central canvas is similar to the *Wilhelm Tell* of the Swiss painter Hodler. Hodler's paintings were hung next to Munch's in the Berlin exhibition of 1902

20 Bibl. 78, p. 18

21 Bibl. 6, p. 21

22 Bibl. 106

23 Bibl. 6, p. 47

24 In repetitions of earlier paintings the earlier devices are usually repeated

25 Pola Gauguin cites the fact that Munch, in about 1935, wrote concerning the years of his early life and referred specifically to his relation to Karsten. Bibl. 16, 2d ed. pp. 301 f.

26 Bibl. 4, pp. 1 ff.

60

60 NUDE BY THE ARM CHAIR 1929

Paintings

Edvard Munch in his open air studio

1

1 THE HOSPITAL WARD 1881

65

2

3

2 SELF-PORTRAIT 1882

3 INGER MUNCH IN BLACK 1884

5 THE EVENING HOUR 1888

6 SPRING DAY ON THE KARL JOHAN 1891

8   KISS BY THE WINDOW 1891

9   INGER MUNCH 1892

E.Munch 1892

9

10

11

10 DAGNY JUELL PRZYBYSZEWSKI 1893
11 THE CRY 1893

12

12 VAMPIRE 1893–94

13 MADONNA 1894

13

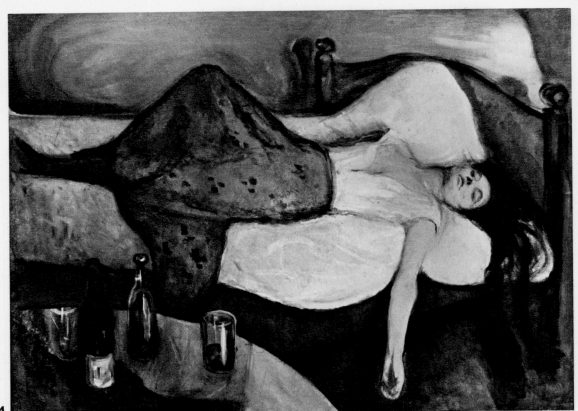

14

14 THE DAY AFTER 1894

15 PUBERTY 1894

16

16 ASHES 1894

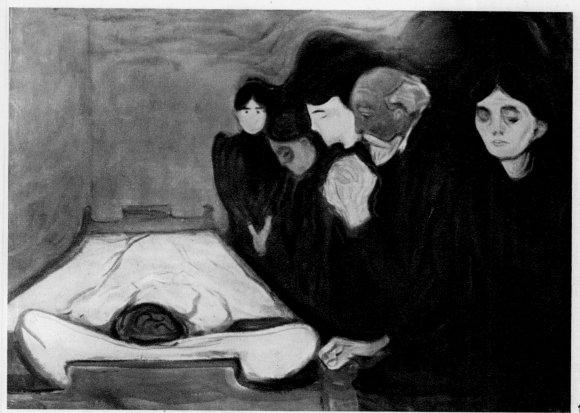

18

18 BY THE DEATH BED 1895

19

19 JEALOUSY 1895 (?)

21

21 IN HELL 1895

23

24

23 NUDE ON A RED BACKGROUND 1896

24 INHERITANCE 1897–99

25

25 THE DANCE OF LIFE 1899–1900

26 THE RED-HAIRED NUDE c.1900

27 THE RED VINE 1900

28

28 MELANCHOLIA 1900

31

31 TRAIN SMOKE 1901

32

32 WHITE NIGHT 1901

33

33 FOUR LITTLE GIRLS OF AASGAARDSTRAND 1903

35

35 THE GARDEN WALL 1904

36

36 PEOPLE ON THE BEACH 1904

38

38 SELF-PORTRAIT WITH A WINE BOTTLE 1906

39

39 MARAT'S DEATH 1906

41 WALTER RATHENAU 1907

41

42

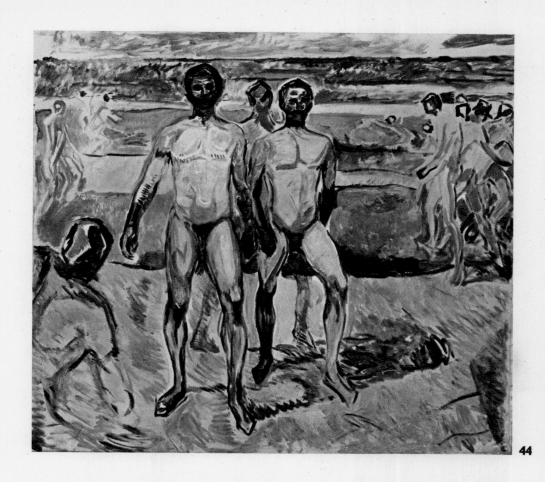

44

42 TWO WORKMEN 1908

44 THE BATHERS TRIPTYCH: MANHOOD 1907–13

97

46

46 DR. DANIEL
JACOBSON 1909

47 THORVALD
STANG 1909

47

48 WINTER LANDSCAPE WITH A PINE TREE 1912

49

49 GALLOPING HORSE *1912*

50

50 THE SUN 1912

51

51 WORKMEN COMING HOME 1915

52

53

52 SELF-PORTRAIT WITH THE NEW CHURCH, BERGEN 1916

53 SELF-PORTRAIT—SPANISH INFLUENZA 1919

56

56 STARRY NIGHT 1923

57

57 THE SICK CHILD 1926

58

58 MODEL ON THE SOFA 1925–26–1928

61

61 UNWELCOME GUESTS 1935

62

62 THE FIGHT 1935

63

63 SELF-PORTRAIT BETWEEN THE CLOCK AND THE BED 1940

64 SELF-PORTRAIT 1942

Catalog of the Exhibition

†*Paintings marked thus are included for reference, but are not illustrated. Measurements are in inches, height precedes width.*

Paintings

1 *The Hospital Ward* 1881
26½″ × 23″, Oslo Municipal Collections

2 *Self-Portrait* 1882
10¼″ × 7½″, Inger Munch, Oslo

3 *Inger Munch in Black* 1884
38″ × 26½″, National Gallery, Oslo

† 4 *Tête-à-Tête* 1885
26½″ × 30½″, Oslo Municipal Collections

5 *The Evening Hour* 1888
29¼″ × 39½″, Thorvald Johnsen, Oslo

6 *Spring Day on the Karl Johan* 1891
34¾″ × 39¼″, Gallery of Painting, Bergen

† 7 *Evening—The Yellow Boat* 1891
25½″ × 37½″, Christian Mustad, Oslo

8 *Kiss by the Window* 1892
28½″ × 35¾″, Christian Mustad, Oslo

9 *Inger Munch* 1892
67¾″ × 48¼″, National Gallery, Oslo

10 *Dagny Juell Przybyszewski* 1893
59″ × 39½″, Oslo Municipal Collections

11 *The Cry* 1893
33″ × 26½″, Oslo Municipal Collections

12 *Vampire* 1893–94
35¾″ × 43″, Oslo Municipal Collections

13 *Madonna* 1894
35½″ × 27″, Oslo Municipal Collections

14 *The Day After* 1894
45¼″ × 59¾″, National Gallery, Oslo

15 *Puberty* 1894
59″ × 43¾″, National Gallery, Oslo

16 *Ashes* 1894
47½″ × 55½″, National Gallery, Oslo

17 *Anxiety* 1894
37½″ × 28¾″, Oslo Municipal Collections

18 *By the Death Bed* 1895
35¾″ × 48¼″, Rasmus Meyer Collection, Bergen

19 *Jealousy* 1895(?)
25½″ × 39″, Rasmus Meyer Collection, Bergen

†20 *Self-Portrait Under the Mask* 1895
27½″ × 17½″, Oslo Municipal Collections

21 *In Hell* 1895
32¼″ × 26″, Oslo Municipal Collections

22 *Self-Portrait with a Cigarette* 1895
43¼″ × 33¾″, National Gallery, Oslo

23 *Nude on a Red Background* 1896
31½″ × 23½″, Christian Mustad, Oslo

24 *Inheritance* 1897–99
55½″ × 47½″, Oslo Municipal Collections

25 *The Dance of Life* 1899–1900
49¼″ × 75″, National Gallery, Oslo

26 *The Red-Haired Nude* c. 1900
47½″ × 19″, Oslo Municipal Collections

27 *The Red Vine* 1900
47¼″ × 46¾″, Oslo Municipal Collections

28 *Melancholia* 1900
43½″ × 49¼″, Oslo Municipal Collections

†29 *The Island* 1901
37¾″ × 41¾″, A. M. Vik, Oslo

30 *Girls on the Bridge* 1901
53½″ × 49½″, National Gallery, Oslo

31 *Train Smoke* 1901
33″ × 43″, J. Cappelen, Oslo

32 *White Night* 1901
45½″ × 43½″, National Gallery, Oslo

33 *Four Little Girls of Aasgaardstrand* 1903
34¼″ × 43¾″, Oslo Municipal Collections

34 *Boys, Girls and Ducks* 1903
39½″ × 41¾″, Oslo Municipal Collections

35 *The Garden Wall* 1904
38¼″ × 40½″, J. B. Stang, Oslo

36 *People on the Shore* 1904
35½″ × 68½″, Oslo Municipal Collections

†37 *Adam and Eve* 1906(?)
52″ × 80″, Oslo Municipal Collections

38 *Self-Portrait with a Wine Bottle* 1906
43¼″ × 47¼″, Oslo Municipal Collections

39 *Marat's Death* 1906
59″ × 78¾″, Oslo Municipal Collections

†40 *Standing Nude* 1907
68½″ × 23¼″, Oslo Municipal Collections

41 *Walter Rathenau* 1907
86½″ × 43¼″, Rasmus Meyer Collection, Bergen

42 *Two Workmen* 1908
35¾″ × 27½″, Oslo Municipal Collections

†43 *The Bathers Triptych: Youth* 1907–13
80¾″ × 38¼″, Oslo Municipal Collections

44 *The Bathers Triptych: Manhood* 1907–13
80″ × 90½″, Oslo Municipal Collections

†45 *The Bathers Triptych: Old Age* 1907–13
78¾″ × 37¾″, Oslo Municipal Collections

46 *Dr. Daniel Jacobson* 1909
80¼″ × 41¼″, Oslo Municipal Collections

47 *Thorvald Stang* 1909
79½″ × 38½″, Oslo Municipal Collections

48 *Winter Landscape with a Pine Tree* 1912
51¾″ × 51½″, Oslo Municipal Collections

49 *Galloping Horse* 1912
58¼″ × 47¼″, Oslo Municipal Collections

50 *The Sun* 1912
48½″ × 69¾″, Oslo Municipal Collections

51 *Workmen Coming Home* 1915
78¾″ × 89¼″, Oslo Municipal Collections

52 *Self-Portrait with the New Church, Bergen* 1916
35½″ × 23½″, Oslo Municipal Collections

53 *Self-Portrait—Spanish Influenza* 1919
59¼″ × 51½″, National Gallery, Oslo

†54 *Under the Horse-Chestnut Tree* 1920
46″ × 47¼″, Oslo Municipal Collections

55 *On the Veranda* 1923
35¼″ × 30″, Oslo Municipal Collections

56 *Landscape with a Starry Sky* 1923
55″ × 47¼″, Oslo Municipal Collections

57 *The Sick Child* 1926
45¾″ × 46″, Oslo Municipal Collections

58 *Model on the Sofa* 1925–26–28
54″ × 45¼″, Oslo Municipal Collections

†59 *Nude* 1926
70″ × 23¼″, Oslo Municipal Collections

60 *Nude by the Armchair* 1929
47¼″ × 39¼″, Oslo Municipal Collections

61 *Unwelcome Guests* 1935
30″ × 39¾″, Oslo Municipal Collections

62 *The Fight* 1935
41¼″ × 47¼″, Oslo Municipal Collections

63 *Self-Portrait Between the Clock and the Bed* 1940
59″ × 47¼″, Oslo Municipal Collections

64 *Self-Portrait* 1942
41¼″ × 25½″, Oslo Municipal Collections

Watercolors

65 *Boys Playing* c. 1912
18″ × 24¾″, R. Moltzau, Oslo

66 *The Blue Hat* 1917
13½″ × 10″, R. Moltzau, Oslo

67 *Red Barn* c. 1920
19¼″ × 25¼″, R. Moltzau, Oslo

68 *The Anemone Hill* c. 1920
19¼″ × 25½″, R. Moltzau, Oslo

69 *Two Nudes* c. 1920
19¼″ × 24¾″, R. Moltzau, Oslo

Etchings *

70 *Maiden and Death* 1894. Drypoint
11½″ × 8¼″ Sch. 3, IIb

71 *Consolation* 1894. Drypoint and aquatint
8¼″ × 12⅛″ Sch. 6, IIIb

72 *The Sick Child* 1894. Drypoint
14¼″ × 10⅝″ Sch. 7, Vd

73 *Christiania Bohemia I* 1895. Etching and aquatint
8⅛″ × 11⅜″ Sch. 10, IId

74 *Moonlight* 1895. Drypoint and aquatint
12¼″ × 9⅞″ Sch. 13, IIId

75 *Bathing Women* 1895. Drypoint and aquatint
8⅜″ × 12¼″ Sch. 14, I

76 *Summer Night* 1895. Drypoint and aquatint
9⅜″ × 12⅜″ Sch. 19, IIb

77 *The Kiss* 1895. Drypoint and aquatint
13″ × 10⅜″ Sch. 22, b

78 *Portrait of a Young Girl* 1895. Drypoint
13¼″ × 9⅞″ Sch. 38, II

79 *Reclining Nude* 1896. Zincograph
8½″ × 11⅜″ Sch. 41, a

80 *Maiden and the Heart* 1896. Etching
9⅜″ × 9⅜″ Sch. 48, b

81 *Boys Swimming* 1897. Colored zincograph
11¾″ × 9⅜″ Sch. 85, b

82 *Helge Rode* 1898. Drypoint
10¼″ × 7⅝″ Sch. 103, II

83 *Miss Ch.* (*The Nurse*) 1908. Drypoint
8⅛″ × 6″ Sch. 269, IIb

84 *Standing Nude* 1913. Etching
19⅜″ × 9⅝″ Sch. 393

85 *In Secret* 1913. Etching
6¼″ × 9⅜″ Sch. 403

Lithographs

86 *Self-Portrait* 1895
17⅞″ × 12½″ Sch. 31

87 *The Cry* 1895
13¾″ × 9⅞″ Sch. 32

88 *Madonna* 1895–1902. In color
23⅞″ × 17⅜″ Sch. 33, A IIb

89 *Vampire* 1895–1902. Lithograph and colored woodcut 15″ × 21⅝″ Sch. 34, IIb

90 *Tingel-Tangel* 1895
16⅛″ × 24¾″ Sch. 37

91 *Jealousy* 1896
12⅞″ × 18⅛″ Sch. 57

92 *The Sick Child* 1896. In color
16⅝″ × 22¼″ Sch. 59, d

††93 *Anxiety* 1896 In color
16½″ × 15⅛″ Sch. 61, b II

94 *The Urn* 1896
18⅛″ × 8⅛″ Sch. 63, II

95 *Attraction* 1896
18⅝″ × 14″ Sch. 65

96 *Separation* 1896
19¼″ × 23″ Sch. 67

97 *Separation* 1896
16⅜″ × 25″ Sch. 68, a

98 *The Lovers* 1896
12¼″ × 16½″ Sch. 71

99 *The Death Chamber* 1896
15½″ × 21½″ Sch. 73

100 *August Strindberg* 1896
24″ × 18⅛″ Sch. 77, II

101 *Stéphane Mallarmé* 1896
20½″ × 11⅝″ Sch. 79, b

102 *Woman and the Urn* 1898
16½″ × 11⅝″ Sch. 104

103 *Stanislas Przybyszewski* 1898
21⅜″ × 17⅜″ Sch. 105

104 *Burlesque Loving Pair* 1898
11⅞″ × 14⅜″ Sch. 106

105 *Lust* 1898
11⅝″ × 17⅞″ Sch. 108

106 "*Good Evening, Good Evening*" 1899
16⅜″ × 20⅞″ Sch. 121

* The prints are the property of the Oslo Municipal Collections.
The numbers preceded by *Sch.* refer to Gustav Schiefler, *Das Graphische Werk*, Bibl. 170, 176.
Nat. Gal. refers to the catalog of the National Gallery, Oslo, *Edvard Munch's Tresnitt*, 1946.
Uncataloged prints are referred to by the inventory number of the Oslo Municipal Collections.

†† This print is lent by the Museum of Modern Art, New York.

107 *Woman* 1899
$18\frac{1}{4}'' \times 23\frac{1}{4}''$ Sch. 122
108 *Flight* c. 1899–1900
$16\frac{1}{2}'' \times 11\frac{3}{4}''$ No. 446
109 *Harpy* 1900. In color
$14\frac{3}{8}'' \times 12\frac{5}{8}''$ Sch. 137, b
110 *Nude with Red Hair* 1901. In color
$19\frac{1}{2}'' \times 15\frac{1}{2}''$ Sch. 142, c
111 *Ibsen in the Grand Café* 1902
$16\frac{7}{8}'' \times 23\frac{1}{4}''$ Sch. 171
112 *The Violin Concert* 1903
$18\frac{1}{2}'' \times 19\frac{3}{4}''$ Sch. 211, II
113 *Madonna (The Brooch)* 1903
$23\frac{3}{8}'' \times 18\frac{1}{4}''$ Sch. 212
114 *Albert Kollmann* 1906
$17\frac{1}{8}'' \times 13\frac{3}{8}''$ Sch. 244
115 *Andreas Schwarz* 1906
$11\frac{5}{8}'' \times 8\frac{5}{8}''$ Sch. 251
116 *Berlin Girl* 1906. In color
$16\frac{7}{8}'' \times 13\frac{3}{8}''$ Sch. 253, II
117 *Nude in Interior* 1907
$15\frac{1}{2}'' \times 14\frac{1}{2}''$ No. 540
118 *Fru Helge Rode* 1908–09
$17\frac{7}{8}'' \times 13\frac{3}{8}''$ Sch. 280, c
119 *Omega and the Tiger* 1908–09
$12\frac{1}{4}'' \times 14\frac{3}{4}''$ Sch. 316
120 *Alpha's Despair* 1908–09
$16\frac{1}{2}'' \times 13''$ Sch. 325
121 *Nude from the Back* 1912
$16\frac{1}{2}'' \times 16\frac{3}{4}''$ Sch. 376, a
122 *Lion* 1912
$7\frac{1}{8}'' \times 12''$ Sch. 384
123 *Snow Shovelers* 1912. Lithograph and woodcut
$25\frac{1}{2}'' \times 20\frac{5}{8}''$ Sch. 385, b
124 *Self-Portrait—Dance of Death* 1915
$19\frac{1}{4}'' \times 11\frac{5}{8}''$ Sch. 432, I
125 *The Lion Tamer* 1916
$19\frac{1}{4}'' \times 25\frac{3}{4}''$ Sch. 456, b
126 *Head of a Woman with Hand to Her Mouth* 1920
$15'' \times 10\frac{5}{8}''$ Sch. 481
127 *Death of the Bohemian* 1927
$10\frac{1}{4}'' \times 15\frac{1}{2}''$ No. 538
128 *Professor K. E. Schreiner* 1930
$23\frac{3}{4}'' \times 20''$ No. 554
129 *Birgitte* 1931
$16\frac{1}{2}'' \times 12\frac{3}{4}''$ No. 535
130 *Self-Portrait Wearing a Hat* 1932
$9\frac{7}{8}'' \times 7\frac{1}{2}''$ No. 456

Woodcuts

131 *Anxiety* 1896. In color
$18\frac{1}{8}'' \times 14\frac{7}{8}''$ Sch. 62
132 *Moonlight* 1896–1901. In color
$16\frac{1}{4}'' \times 18\frac{5}{8}''$ Sch. 81, B
133 *In the Man's Brain* 1897
$14\frac{3}{4}'' \times 22\frac{5}{8}''$ Sch. 98
134 *Nude from the Back* 1897
$15\frac{5}{8}'' \times 6\frac{1}{4}''$ Sch. 99
135 *The Kiss (First State)* 1897
$23\frac{1}{4}'' \times 18''$ Sch. 102, A
136 *The Kiss (Fourth State)* 1897–1902
$18\frac{3}{8}'' \times 18\frac{1}{4}''$ Sch. 102, D
137 *Salome* 1898
$17\frac{3}{4}'' \times 12\frac{1}{4}''$ Sch. 109
138 *Blood Blossom* 1898
$18\frac{1}{8}'' \times 12\frac{7}{8}''$ Sch. 114 Black on white

139 *Women on the Shore* 1898. In color
$17\frac{7}{8}'' \times 20''$ Sch. 117, b
140 *Winter Landscape* 1898
$12\frac{1}{4}'' \times 18''$ Sch. 118, a
141 *Head of a Woman* 1898(?)
$17\frac{1}{4}'' \times 13\frac{1}{4}''$ Nat. Gal. 85
142 *Old Fisherman* 1899
$17\frac{1}{4}'' \times 14''$ Sch. 124 II
143 *Shore, Sea and Moon* 1899. In color
$14\frac{3}{4}'' \times 22\frac{1}{2}''$ Sch. 125, b
144 *Nude Man on the Shore* 1899. In color
$17\frac{1}{2}'' \times 17\frac{1}{2}''$ Sch. 126
145 *Boy Bathers* 1899–1917. In color
$14\frac{1}{2}'' \times 17\frac{1}{2}''$ Sch. 127. Nat. Gal. 26
146 *Girl Bather* 1899
$16\frac{5}{8}'' \times 20\frac{5}{8}''$ Sch. 128
147 *Girl's Head Against the Shore* 1899. In color
$18\frac{1}{4}'' \times 16\frac{1}{4}''$ Sch. 129, a
148 *Woman's Head* 1899. In color
$10'' \times 7\frac{1}{4}''$ Sch. 130
149 *The Fat Prostitute* 1899. In color
$9\frac{7}{8}'' \times 7\frac{7}{8}''$ Sch. 131, b
150 *Man and Woman* 1899. In color
$16\frac{1}{2}'' \times 20''$ Sch. 132
151 *Two Beings (The Lonely Ones)* 1899–1917. In color
$15\frac{1}{2}'' \times 22''$ Sch. 133. Nat. Gal. 32 A
152 *Two Beings (The Lonely Ones)* 1899–1917. In color
$15\frac{1}{2}'' \times 21\frac{1}{4}''$ Sch. 133. Nat. Gal. 32 B
153 *Kneeling Woman* 1899
$20\frac{1}{2}'' \times 16\frac{1}{2}''$ Sch. 133, a
154 *Old Man Praying* 1902. In color
$18'' \times 12\frac{3}{4}''$ Sch. 173
155 *Man and Woman Kissing* 1904
$15\frac{3}{4}'' \times 21\frac{1}{4}''$ Sch. 230, a
156 *Man and Woman* 1904
$9\frac{7}{8}'' \times 7\frac{3}{4}''$ Sch. 231
157 *Woman's Head* 1904
$9\frac{7}{8}'' \times 7\frac{3}{4}''$ Sch. 234
158 *Old Men and Boys* 1904
$13\frac{3}{8}'' \times 17\frac{3}{8}''$ Sch. 235
159 *Old Man* 1904
$26\frac{3}{4}'' \times 17\frac{7}{8}''$ Sch. 237
160 *Self-Portrait* 1911
$21\frac{5}{8}'' \times 13\frac{5}{8}''$ Sch. 352
161 *Young Girl on the Shore* 1912. In color
$7\frac{1}{2}'' \times 10''$ Sch. 387, b
162 *Rocky Cliffs and Sea* 1912
$12\frac{5}{8}'' \times 23\frac{5}{8}''$ Sch. 389
163 *Sun Bather* 1915. In color
$13\frac{7}{8}'' \times 22''$ Sch. 440, b
164 *Lovers in Pine Woods* 1915. In color
$12\frac{5}{8}'' \times 23\frac{5}{8}''$ Sch. 442
165 *To the Wood* 1915. In color
$20\frac{5}{8}'' \times 25\frac{5}{8}''$ Sch. 444
166 *Girls on the Bridge* 1920. Woodcut and colored
lithograph $19\frac{5}{8}'' \times 16\frac{5}{8}''$ Sch. 488, b Nat. Gal. 78
167 *The Last Hour* 1920
$16\frac{1}{4}'' \times 22\frac{5}{8}''$ Sch. 491
168 *Standing Nude* c. 1925
$26\frac{3}{4}'' \times 13\frac{3}{4}''$ Nat. Gal. 111
169 *The Trial by Fire* c. 1927
$18\frac{1}{4}'' \times 14\frac{1}{4}''$ Nat. Gal. 89
170 *Birgitte* 1931. In color
$18\frac{1}{4}'' \times 14\frac{1}{4}''$ Nat. Gal. 134 A
171 Wood Block for *Two Beings*
Nos. 151, 152

Selected
Bibliography

This bibliography comprises a list of the artist's writings and selected references to the most significant critical and biographical information on Munch which has been published in books and periodicals during the last 57 years; the earliest item noted is dated 1892. Newspaper notices, some of which doubtless appeared before that time, and which have continued through the years to provide undistilled comment and immediate reaction to the artist's work, have not been cited; nor have exhibition catalogs and exhibition reviews (with the exception of a few longer critical articles) been included.

Munch bibliographies have been compiled earlier by Glaser (bibl. 28); by Langaard (bibl. 50), and by Hodin (bibl. 39); bibliographical essays have been written by Nygård-Nilssen and Wartmann. An exhaustive bibliography and an almost complete listing of Munch exhibitions with relevant literature has been prepared by this compiler and is on file in the Museum of Modern Art Library.

Because Munch and his work have been best known in the Scandinavian countries and in Germany, the major portion of the material concerning him has been written in the languages of those countries. For assistance in the interpretation of Scandinavian material in the preparation of this bibliography, the compiler is indebted to Miss Anne Bollman of the Museum of Modern Art Library staff.

The arrangement of the bibliography is alphabetical by the author's name, or by title in the case of a book or article with many contributors, or of an unsigned article. Munch's own writings have been arranged chronologically.

The following abbreviations and symbols have been used: Ap April, Ag August, Aufl. Auflage (edition) Bd. Band (volume), col colored, D December, F February, hft Heft (number), il illustration(s), Ja January, Je June, Jy July, Mr March, My May, N November, no number(s), [n.d.] not dated, O October, p page(s), S September, ser series, sup supplementary, v volume, [   ] title supplied by the compiler.

For brevity, the designations *volume* and *page* have not been used in periodical references. Thus, the reference Der Cicerone (Leipzig) 15hft14:632-4 Jy 1923 means that the article may be found in volume 15, number 14, pages 632-634 of that magazine for July 1923.

Hannah B. Muller
Assistant Librarian
The Museum of Modern Art, New York

1 BIERMANN, GEORG. Edvard Munchs graphische Kunst. il Der Cicerone (Leipzig) 15hft14:632-4 Jy 1923.
Also published in Jahrbuch der Jungen Kunst (Leipzig) 4:392-5 1923

2 DERI, MAX. Die Malerei im XIX. Jahrhundert. 1:415-37 il Berlin, Cassirer, 1923.
Includes analyses of 16 works by Munch

3 EDVARD MUNCH I TYSK KUNSTKRITIKK. Kunst og Kultur (Bergen) 14:111-28 1927.
Articles by the German critics: Meier-Graefe; Paul Westheim (first published in his Helden und Abenteurer. p167-71 Berlin, Reckendorf, 1931); Otto H. Förster; Karl Scheffler (first published in his Talente 2. Aufl. p195-203 Berlin, Cassirer, 1919)

4 EDVARD MUNCH: MENNESKET OG KUNSTNEREN. 162p il Oslo, Gyldendal Norsk Forlag, 1946. (Kunst og kulturs serie.)
Edvard Munch: the man and the artist. Contributions (reprinted from Kunst og Kultur (Bergen) 29hft3-4: 73-232 1946) by Karl Stenerud, Axel L. Romdahl, Pola Gauguin, Christian Gierløff, N. Rygg, Erik Pedersen, Birgit Prestøe, Chrix Dahl, Johan H. Langaard

5 EDVARD MUNCH OG JAPPE NILSSEN: EFTERLATTE BREV OG KRITIKKER. 118p il Oslo, Dreyers Forlag, 1946.
Correspondence between Edvard Munch and Jappe Nilssen; Nilssen's criticism of Munch exhibitions, 1911, 1912, 1927, and his "Dekorasjonene på Freia chokoladefabrik" which was published in Oslo, 1922. Introduction by Erna Holmboe Bang

6 EDVARD MUNCH SOM VI KJENTE HAM: VENNENE FORTELLER. 221p il Oslo, Dreyers Forlag, 1946.
Edvard Munch as we knew him: told by his friends.
Contributions by K. E. Schreiner, Johs. Roede, Ingeborg Motzfeldt Løchen, Titus Vibe Müller, Birgit Prestøe, David Bergendahl (on Munch's lithographs), Christian Gierløff, Pola Gauguin (on Munch exhibition in Bergen, 1909; with correspondence from Munch to Sigurd Høst), L. O. Ravensberg

7 EKELÖF, GUNNAR. Edvard Munch. Reflexioner med anledning av utställningen i Konstakademien, Stockholm. il Konstrevy (Stockholm) 13:79–83 1937.
Occasioned by Munch exhibition, Stockholm, 1936

8 ESSWEIN, HERMANN. Edvard Munch. 46p il München und Leipzig, R. Piper, 1905. (Moderne Illustratoren. Bd. 7.)
List of prints available for sale at R. Piper, with prices, p4–6; résumé of bibl. 66, p23–4

9 FÅHRAEUS, KLAS. Edvard Munch. il Konstrevy (Stockholm) p2–14 1927.
An analysis of his life and work as related to his country and his time

10 FRAENGER, WILHELM. Zu einem Selbstbildnis von Edvard Munch. il Der Cicerone (Leipzig) 12hft23:837–40 1920.
Also published in Jahrbuch der Jungen Kunst (Leipzig) 2:21–5 1921

11 FRIEDEBERGER, HANS. Gelegentlich einer Ausstellung Munchscher Werke im Kunstsalon Gurlitt in Berlin. il Der Cicerone (Leipzig) 6hft4:122–7 F 1914

12 FRIEDLÄNDER, MAX J. Über Edvard Munch. il Kunst für Alle (Munich) 31:337–46 Je 1916.
Occasioned by exhibition of Munch's graphic work at J. B. Neumann, Berlin

13 – Zu einer Landschaft Edvard Munchs aus dem Jahre 1917. il Genius (Munich) 3:55–7 1920.
Occasioned by exhibition, Paul Cassirer, Berlin, 1920

14 FUGL, ALEXANDER. Edvard Munch, 70 aar. il Samleren (Copenhagen) 10:165–80 1933.
Chronology, p180

15 – Kronologisk fortegnelse over Edvard Munchs malerier. il Samleren (Copenhagen) 10 N 1933.
A chronological list of Munch's paintings (not complete) from 1880 to 1907. Published without page numbers in special Munch issue

16 GAUGUIN, POLA. Edvard Munch. 281p il Oslo, H. Aschehoug, 1933.
Second edition published in 1946, 320p il

17 – Edvard Munch. il Ord och Bild (Stockholm) 48:9–14 1939

18 – Grafikeren Edvard Munch. 2v il Trondheim, F. Brun, 1946

19 GLASER, CURT. Edvard Munch als Graphiker. il Kunst und Künstler (Berlin) 11:570–8 Ag 1913

20 – Edvard Munchs Wandgemälde für die Universität in Kristiania. il Zeitschrift für Bildende Kunst (Leipzig) neue folge 25:61–6 1914

21 – Edvard Munch. 191p il Berlin, Bruno Cassirer, 1917.
Includes original etching by Munch. Second edition published in 1922, 207p il. A portion of chapter 1: Lebenslauf published in Kunst und Künstler (Berlin) 15:530–9 Ag 1917

22 – Edvard Munchs graphische Kunst. il Das Werk (Bern) 9:159–68 1922

23 – Edvard Munch. Wissen und Leben (Zurich) 15:811–19 Jy 20 1922

24 – Die Graphik der Neuzeit. p517–27 il Berlin, Cassirer, 1923

25 – Edvard Munch. il Der Cicerone (Leipzig) 16no21:1010–19 N 1924.
Introduction to catalog of Munch exhibition, Spring 1924, Neue Galerie, Vienna. Also published in Jahrbuch der Jungen Kunst (Leipzig) 5:206–13 1924

26 – Edvard Munch. il Der Querschnitt (Berlin) 6:924–9 1926

27 – Besuch bei Munch. il Kunst und Künstler (Berlin) 25:203–9 Mr 1927.
Description of Munch's home. Translated into Czech in Volné Sméry (Prague) 25:140–2 1927/8

28 – Munch. In Thieme-Becker. Allgemeines Lexikon der bildenden Künstler 25:265–7. Leipzig, Seemann, 1931.
Includes extensive bibliography

29 HALS, HARALD, II. Edvard Munch og Åsgårdstrand. il Vestfold Minne (Oslo) 5:65–78 1946.
An account of life in that village with photographs of subjects of his paintings

30 HEILBUT, EMIL. Die Sammlung Linde in Lübeck. il Kunst und Künstler (Berlin) 2:303–25 My 1904.
Munch, especially his graphic work, p316–24

31 – Einige neue Bildnisse von Edvard Munch. il Kunst und Künstler (Berlin) 2:489–92 1904.
Analyses of portraits of Graf Kessler, a young Frenchman, and Herman Schlittgen

32 HERMAN, STANISLAS. Stanislas Przybyszewski (de 1868 à 1900). p212–20 Lille, G. Sautai, 1939.
Published as a doctoral thesis, Faculté des lettres de l'Université de Paris. A source of information on Munch's Berlin days

33 HILDEBRANDT, HANS. Die Kunst des 19. und 20. Jahrhunderts. p363–4 il Wildpark-Potsdam, Akademische Verlagsgesellschaft Athenaion, 1924

34 HODIN, J. P. Ett möte med Edvard Munch. il Konstrevy (Stockholm) 15:9–13 1939.
An interview. Includes statements by Munch

35 – August Strindberg om Edvard Munch. il Konstrevy (Stockholm) 16:199–202 1940.
A discussion of Strindberg's article on Munch which appeared in La Revue Blanche, 1896, and which is here reprinted and translated into Swedish

36 – Edvard Munch. il Studio (London) 130:21–4 Jy 1945

37 – Edvard Munch och hans stad. Minnen och intryck från Oslo. il Frihet (Stockholm) 31no6: 15–17 Mr 1947.
Munch and his city. Memories and impressions from Oslo. Includes an extract from Munch's article in St. Hallvard, 1929, on the colors of Norway

38 – Jag skall måla människor, som älskar och lider. il Idun (Stockholm) 60no3:6–7, 21–2 Ja 16 1947.
Hodin interviews Munch's sister and reports her comments on the artist's life and family

39 – Edvard Munch, der Genius des Nordens. 140p il (some col) Stockholm, Neuer Verlag, 1948.
Includes extensive bibliography

40 – Edvard Munch, un génie nordique. il Arts Plastiques (Brussels) no3–4:111–21 1949

41 HUNEKER, JAMES GIBBONS. Ivory, apes and peacocks. p231–5 New York, C. Scribner's, 1932.
Reprinted from New York Times, My 11 1913

42 INGEBRETSEN, ELI. Edvard Munchs grafikk. 20p il Oslo, Nasjonalgalleriet, 1932. (Veileder 5)

43 – Edvard Munchs tresnitt. il Konstrevy (Stockholm) 22:182–5 1946.
Munch's woodcuts. Occasioned by exhibition, Nasjonalgalleriet, Oslo

44 JOHNSON, ELLEN. Development of Edvard Munch. il Art Quarterly (Detroit) 10no2:86–9 1947

45 JUSTI, LUDWIG. Von Corinth bis Klee. p109–16 il Berlin, Julius Bard, 1931 (Deutsche Malerkunst im 19. und 20. Jahrhundert).
Includes analyses of Munch's paintings in the Nationalgalerie, Berlin

46 KROHG, CHRISTIAN. Kampen for tilvaerelsen. 1: 186–205 il København, Gyldendalske Boghandel Nordisk Forlag, 1920.
Writings by Munch's teacher dated 1889, 1891, 1902, 1912. Includes comments on Munch's painting Evening and on his sketches for the Oslo mural

47 KUHL, GUSTAV. Edvard Munch. Sozialistische Monatshefte (Berlin) 7:440–4 1903

48 KUNST OG KULTUR (Bergen) il 4hft2:66–128 1913.
Special Munch number. Includes contributions by Jens Thiis, Jappe Nilssen, Christian Gierløff, Sigurd Høst, Richard Bergh, Ernest Thiel, Curt Glaser, Franz Servaes, Gustav Schiefler, Andrew Levinson, Walther Halvorsen, E. Leistikow (on mural decorations exhibited at Berlin Secession)

KUNST OG KULTUR (Bergen). Special Munch number, 1946. See 4

49 LANGAARD, JOHAN, H. Edvard Munch, maleren. 24p il Oslo, Nasjonalgalleriet, 1932. (Veileder 4)

50 – Les pays scandinaves: la Norvège et le Danemark. il Amour de l'Art (Paris) 15:406–11 1934. Munch, p406–7, 410. Includes extensive bibliography. Reprinted in René Huyghe. Histoire de l'art contemporain: la peinture, Paris, Alcan, 1935

51 – Edvard Munch. A splendid bequest to the city of Oslo. il American Scandinavian Review (New York) 33:220–7 D 1945

52 – 5 malerier av Edvard Munch. il Statens Museum for Kunst, Copenhagen. Kunstmuseets Aarsskrift 33–4:81–98 1946–7.
Analysis of Aftenpassiar, 1889, Dødskamp, 1915, Hjemvendende Arbeidere, 1919, Daniel Jacobson, 1908, Portrett av Svartkledd Dame, c.1892

53 – Edvard Munchs selvportretter. 161p il Oslo, Gyldendal Norsk Forlag, 1947

54 – Edvard Munchs formler: et lite forsøk på en formanalyse. il Samtiden (Oslo) p50–6 1948.
Edvard Munch's formulas: an attempt at a form analysis

55 LEISTIKOW, W. (Walter Selber, pseud.). Die Affaire Munch. Freie Bühne (Berlin) 3:1296–1300 1892.
Discussion of Munch's first Berlin exhibition, 1892

56 LINDE, MAX. Edvard Munch und die Kunst der Zukunft. 15p il (some col) Berlin, Gottheiner, 1902.
Contains original color print. New edition published 1905 has two additional illustrations, illustrated title page and color illustration which appears on cover of 1st edition here precedes the text. List of Munch's published etchings on last page of both editions

57 LUND, IDA K. Edvard Munch. il Parnassus (New York) 9no3:21–4 Mr 1937

58 MEIER-GRAEFE, JULIUS. Modern art. 2:73–4 il New York, Putnam, London, Heinemann, 1908. Munch compared to Lautrec, Gauguin, Van Gogh

59 – Entwicklungsgeschichte der modernen Kunst. 2. Aufl. 3:645–53 il München, Piper, 1915

60 NEUMEYER, ALFRED. Edward Munch. il Magazine of Art (Washington, D. C.) 37:263–7 N 1944. Discussion of Munch's work, including his prints

61 NILSSEN, JAPPE. Edvard Munch: A/S Freia Chokoladefabriks Spisesalsdekorasjon. il Kristiania, 1922. An essay on the decorations executed by Munch for the Freia factory restaurant, with reproductions of all the paintings. Text reprinted in bibl. 5

62 NORDENFALK, CARL. Apropos Munch utställningen. il Konstperspektiv (Stockholm) 3no1:3–7 1947. Occasioned by exhibition, Stockholm, 1947

63 NYGÅRD-NILSSEN, ARNE. Munch-litteraturen. il Kunst og Kultur (Bergen) 20:59–64 1934. A bibliographical essay covering important articles on Munch and writings by Munch

64 OSBORN, MAX. Edvard Munch. il Kunst für Alle (Munich) 35:321–32 Je 1920

65 ØVERLAND, ARNULF. Edvard Munch. 67p il Kristiania, Berg & Høghs [192 ?] (Norske kunstnere)

66 PRZYBYSZEWSKI, STANISLAW. Das Werk von Edvard Munch. Vier Beiträge von Stanislaw Przybyszewski, Franz Servaes, Willy Pastor, Julius Meier-Graefe. 95p Berlin, S. Fischer, 1894

67 READ, HERBERT. The significance of Edvard Munch. In the author's Art Now. p84–7 New York, Harcourt Brace, 1934. Also in new edition, London, Faber and Faber, 1948, p78–81, and in The Norseman (London) 1:428–30 N 1943

68 RITTER, WILLIAM. Correspondance de Bohème. Gazette des Beaux Arts (Paris) 2:336–46 1905. Includes unenthusiastic comment on Munch exhibition, Manès gallery, 1905

69 ROMDAHL, AXEL. Edvard Munch. Konst (Stockholm) 2no4:35–7 N 15 1912

70 – Edvard Munch. Intryck och minnen. il Konsthistorisk Tidskrift (Stockholm) 13:41–9 Je 1944

71 – Edvard Munch som expressionist. il Tidskrift för Konstvetenskap (Stockholm) 1947: 165–86

72 SARVIG, OLE. Edvard Munchs graphik. 303p il (some col) København, J. H. Schultz, 1948. Contains the largest number of illustrations of Munch's prints. Also includes interpretative text and bibliography

73 SCHEFFLER, KARL. Edvard Munch. il Kunst und Künstler (Berlin) 12:415–24 My 1914. Illustrates work shown at exhibition, Galerie Fritz Gurlitt

74 SCHIEFLER, GUSTAV. Verzeichnis des graphischen Werks Edvard Munchs bis 1906. 147p il Berlin, Cassirer, 1907. Definitive catalog of Munch's prints. See also bibl. 78. Head and tail pieces and vignettes by Munch

75 – Edvard Munchs Alfa og Omega. il Kunst und Künstler (Berlin) 8:409–13 My 1910

76 – Edvard Munch. Vortrag in der Gesellschaft Hamburgischer Kunstfreunde. 13p Berlin, Verlag des Graphischen Kabinetts J. B. Neumann, 1916. Reprinted with some changes in Das Kunstblatt (Weimar) 1:9–18 Ja 1917. Comments on Munch's life, work, personality. He is compared to Liebermann

77 – Edvard Munchs graphische Kunst. 22p il Dresden, Arnold, 1923. (Arnolds graphische Bücher)

78 – Edvard Munch, das graphische Werk, 1906–1926. 175p il Berlin, Euphorion Verlag, 1928. Definitive catalog of Munch's prints. See also bibl. 74

79 SCHINNERER, ADOLF. Edvard Munch, der Maler. il (some col) Kunst für Alle (Munich) 42:72–81 D 1926

80 – Zu den Bildern von Edvard Munch. il Die Kunst (Munich) 71:131–40 1934

81 SOISSONS, GUY JEAN RAOUL, COMTE DE. Edvard Munch. In the author's The aesthetic purpose of the renaissance and other essays. p105–23 London, Murray and Evenden [1914]. Reprinted from the Fortnightly Review 96:336–46 Ag 1911

82 SPRINGER, JARO. Die freie Berliner Kunstausstellung. Kunst für Alle (Munich) 8:314–15 My 15 1893. The author denounces the jury which rejected Munch's pictures at the Verein der Berliner Künstler exhibition. Other comments on the exhibition in the same volume: p89, D 15 1892; p122 Ja 1 1893; p252 My 15 1893; p363 il S 1 1893

83 STENERSEN, ROLF. Edvard Munch: närbild av ett geni. 220p il Stockholm, Wahlström & Widstrand, 1944. A personal account of Munch by one of his friends and collectors. Includes anecdotal material, and reports of conversations with Munch, including statements by the artist. First published in Norwegian. Also published in German, 171p il (some col) Zürich, Büchergilde

Gutenberg, 1949. Some anecdotes also published in The Norseman (London) 1:416–28 N 1943

84 STRINDBERG, AUGUSTE. L'exposition d'Edvard Munch. Revue Blanche (Paris) 10:525–6 1896. For comment on this article, see bibl. 35. See also writings by Strindberg for references to Munch

85 THIIS, JENS. Edvard Munch. Et foredrag holdt i anledning af en utstilling af kunstnerens arbeider i Kristiania. il Ord och Bild (Stockholm) 16:533–45 1907. A lecture given on the occasion of an exhibition of the artist's work in Oslo

86 – Edvard Munch. Zeitschrift für Bildende Kunst (Berlin) neue folge 19:133–43 1907. An attempt to touch on the outstanding elements of Munch's work and to explain its philosophy

87 – Kunstutstilling i Köln. il Kunst og Kultur (Oslo) 2:234–7 1911/12

88 – Munch. In Scandinavian Art. p580–91 il New York, American-Scandinavian Foundation, 1922. An appreciation of Munch including analyses of some of his paintings

89 – Le grand peintre de la Norvège: Edvard Munch. il Art Vivant (Paris) 6:990–2, 995 D 1930

90 – Edvard Munch og hans samtid. Slekten, livet og kunsten, geniet. 330p il (some col) Oslo, Gyldendal Norsk Forlag, 1933. An authoritative, comprehensive monograph. Also published in French

91 – Edvard Munch. 103p il (some col) Berlin, Rembrandt Verlag, 1934. "Der leibhaftige Munch" by Erich Büttner, p83–101. The first chapter is reprinted, for the most part, from bibl. 90 and from Samtiden (Oslo) 12:24–30 1901

92 THOMPSON, VANCE. Munch, the Norse artist. il Mlle New York (New York) 1no10:10 Ja 1896. Probably first mention of Munch in American literature

93 TIETZE, HANS. Edvard Munch. il Dedalo (Milan) 8no6:377–93 N 1927

94 TIETZE-CONRAT, E. Edvard Munch. il Graphischen Künste (Vienna) 47:75–88 1924. Discussion of Munch's graphic work

95 VIDALENC, GEORGES. L'Art norvégien contemporain. p108-18 Paris, Alcan, 1921

96 WARTMANN, W. Einleitung. In exhibition catalog, Zürich Kunsthaus. Ausstellung Edvard Munch. piii–xviii Zürich, 1922. Includes bibliographical notes

97 – Albert Kollmann, ein Freund von Edvard Munch. il Werk (Winterthur) 31:138–44 1944. Extracts, including a comment by Munch, from Albert Kollmann: ein Leben für die Kunst, 1921; also notes on portraits of Kollmann by Munch

98 – Edvard Munch, der Graphiker. il (some col) Graphis (Zürich) 1no5/6:3–27 Ja–Mr 1945. Text in English, French, German. The influence on Munch of the literary and artistic figures of his early life

99 [Introduction to catalog of exhibition held at Blomqvists Lokale] Oslo, 1903

100 [Introduction to portfolio of lithographs: Alpha und Omega] Copenhagen, 1909

101 Munchs konkurranseutkast til Universitets festsal, Oslo, 1911. With text by Munch

102 [Sales catalog with text by Munch in Norwegian and German] Oslo, 1914, 8p

103 [Catalog of Munch's graphic work] 14p Oslo [n.d.]. Includes text by Munch reprinted from bibl. 100 in Norwegian and French. Catalog is in Norwegian and German

104 [Catalog of 230 graphic works as shown in exhibition in Sweden] 17 leaves il Oslo, c.1914. No text, captions on illustrations in German

105 [Sales catalog of Munch's work] 20p il Oslo, 1917

106 [Introduction to catalog of exhibition held at Blomqvists Lokale] Oslo, 1918. Munch's text entitled: Livsfrisen, 4p; I anledning kritikken, 7p Oslo, 1918. Issued after exhibition at Blomqvists Lokale had begun, and distributed with its catalog

107 [Introduction to catalog of exhibition held at Blomqvists Lokale] Oslo 1918? Munch's text entitled: Livsfrisens Tilblivelse; Kunst og Natur. il p19

108 [Introduction to catalog of exhibition held at Blomqvists Lokale] Oslo, 1929. Text by Munch entitled: Små utdrag av min dagbok, 1889–1929, 2p

109 Oslos farver. St. Hallvard (Oslo) 7:156 1929. Reprinted in 37

110 Mein Freund Przybyszewski. Pologne Littéraire (Warsaw) 3 D 15 1928. Also published in Oslo Aftenavis no25 1929

111 [Comment on German exhibition in Oslo] Dagbladet (Oslo) 1932

112 Edvard Munchs Brev; Familien. Et utvalg ved Inger Munch. 309p. Oslo, Johan Grundt Tanum, 1949. Correspondence of Munch and members of his family. Edited by Inger Munch. Foreword by Johan H. Langaard.

– See also 6, 34, 37, 83, 97